The Power of Flexibility: How Employers Shape Work/Life Balance

Olivia

Copyright © [2023]

Title: The Power of Flexibility: How Employers Shape Work/Life Balance
Author's: Olivia

All rights reserved. No part of this publication may be reproduced, stored in a retrieval system, or transmitted in any form or by any means, electronic, mechanical, photocopying, recording, or otherwise, without the prior written permission of the publisher or author, except in the case of brief quotations embodied in critical reviews and certain other non-commercial uses permitted by copyright law.

This book was printed and published by [Publisher's: **Olivia**] in [2023]

ISBN:

TABLE OF CONTENT

Chapter 1: The Importance of Work/Life Balance　　　　08

Understanding Work/Life Balance

Defining work/life balance

Benefits of work/life balance for employees

The Role of Employers in Promoting Work/Life Balance

Employer responsibility towards work/life balance

Why employers should prioritize work/life balance

Chapter 2: Creating a Flexible Work Environment　　　　22

Flexible Work Arrangements

Telecommuting and remote work options

Flextime and compressed workweeks

Benefits of Flexibility for Employees

Increased productivity and job satisfaction

Better work/life integration

Chapter 3: Flexible Leave Options 34

Paid Time Off (PTO) Policies

Different types of PTO policies

Guidelines for requesting and utilizing PTO

Parental Leave Policies

Maternity and paternity leave options

Supporting new parents in the workplace

Chapter 4: Supporting Employee Well-being 47

Wellness Programs

Health and fitness initiatives

Mental health support and resources

Work/Life Integration Support

Childcare and eldercare assistance

Flexible scheduling during personal emergencies

Chapter 5: Promoting Work/Life Balance Culture   63

Leadership and Management Support

Leading by example in work/life balance

Training managers to support work/life balance

Communication and Transparency

Open dialogue on work/life balance

Sharing resources and information

Chapter 6: Overcoming Challenges and Obstacles   81

Addressing Workload and Burnout

Strategies for managing heavy workloads

Identifying signs of burnout and seeking support

Overcoming Stigma and Cultural Barriers

Challenging societal norms and expectations

Fostering inclusivity and diversity in work/life balance initiatives

Chapter 7: Sustainable Work/Life Balance   93

Maintaining Work/Life Balance in the Long Term

Strategies for sustaining work/life balance

Adjusting to changing personal and professional circumstances

Measuring the Impact of Work/Life Balance Initiatives

Collecting feedback and evaluating effectiveness

Making improvements based on employee input

Chapter 8: The Future of Work/Life Balance   106

Trends and Innovations in Work/Life Balance

Remote work advancements and technology

Evolving policies and practices

Advocating for Work/Life Balance Rights

Employee rights and legal protections

Collaborating with employers for positive change

Conclusion: Empowering Employees for a Balanced Life   **121**

Chapter 1: The Importance of Work/Life Balance

Understanding Work/Life Balance

In today's fast-paced and demanding world, achieving a healthy work/life balance has become increasingly important. In this subchapter, we will delve into the significance of maintaining a harmonious equilibrium between our personal and professional lives. By understanding the importance of work/life balance, employees can lead more fulfilling lives while excelling in their careers.

Work/life balance refers to the delicate juggling act of allocating time and energy between work-related responsibilities and personal commitments. It encompasses various aspects such as managing time effectively, prioritizing self-care, and nurturing personal relationships. Achieving a healthy work/life balance is crucial as it directly impacts our physical and mental well-being, job satisfaction, and overall happiness.

One of the primary reasons why work/life balance is essential is its positive impact on our health. A well-balanced life allows for sufficient rest, exercise, and recreation, which are vital for maintaining good physical health. By prioritizing personal time and engaging in activities that rejuvenate our mind and body, we can reduce stress levels and prevent burnout. Moreover, a healthy work/life balance promotes better mental health, leading to increased productivity and creativity in the workplace.

Beyond health, work/life balance significantly influences job satisfaction. When individuals are able to allocate time for their personal interests and passions, they feel more fulfilled and motivated in their professional lives. Engaging in activities outside of work not only provides a sense of purpose but also enhances overall job performance. A well-rounded employee who can strike a balance between work and personal life brings fresh perspectives and innovative ideas to the table.

Furthermore, work/life balance plays a pivotal role in nurturing personal relationships. By dedicating quality time to family, friends, and oneself, employees can foster stronger bonds and create lasting memories. Maintaining these connections offers emotional support, reduces feelings of isolation, and contributes to a sense of belonging. A healthy work/life balance allows individuals to be present and engaged in their relationships, leading to greater happiness and fulfillment.

In conclusion, understanding the importance of work/life balance is crucial for employees striving for personal and professional success. It not only positively impacts physical and mental health but also boosts job satisfaction and strengthens personal relationships. By prioritizing work/life balance, individuals can lead more fulfilling lives, excel in their careers, and experience a heightened sense of well-being.

Defining work/life balance

In today's fast-paced and demanding work environment, achieving a healthy work/life balance has become a growing concern for employees. But what exactly does it mean to have a work/life balance? And why is it so crucial for our overall well-being?

Work/life balance refers to the equilibrium between our professional and personal lives, where we are able to allocate time and energy to both areas without feeling overwhelmed or neglecting one in favor of the other. It is about finding harmony in all aspects of our lives, including career, family, health, and personal interests. Striking the right balance allows us to meet our work commitments while still having time for ourselves and our loved ones.

The importance of a healthy work/life balance cannot be overstated. Research consistently shows that individuals who maintain a healthy balance experience higher job satisfaction, better physical and mental health, increased productivity, and improved relationships. On the other hand, those who neglect their personal lives in pursuit of professional success often suffer from burnout, stress, and strained relationships.

A healthy work/life balance enables us to recharge and rejuvenate, leading to increased creativity, motivation, and overall job performance. When we have time to relax, pursue hobbies, exercise, and spend quality time with family and friends, we become more fulfilled in all areas of our lives. This sense of fulfillment spills over into our work, making us more engaged and satisfied with our professional responsibilities.

However, achieving work/life balance requires effort and conscious decision-making. It involves setting boundaries, managing time effectively, and prioritizing our personal needs alongside work demands. Employers play a crucial role in shaping work/life balance by offering flexible work arrangements, promoting a supportive and inclusive culture, and fostering open communication channels.

By acknowledging the importance of work/life balance, employers can create an environment that values the well-being and happiness of their employees. With the right support and resources, employees can find the balance they need to thrive both personally and professionally.

In conclusion, work/life balance is about finding harmony between our work and personal lives, where we can fulfill our professional responsibilities without neglecting our personal well-being. It is a crucial factor in achieving job satisfaction, maintaining good physical and mental health, and nurturing relationships. Employers have the power to shape work/life balance by offering flexible arrangements and fostering a supportive culture. By prioritizing work/life balance, we can create a healthier and more fulfilling work environment for all employees.

Benefits of work/life balance for employees

In today's fast-paced and demanding world, maintaining a healthy work/life balance has become essential for employees to thrive and succeed. The importance of striking a balance between professional and personal lives cannot be overstated. In this subchapter, we will explore the numerous benefits that a work/life balance can bring to employees.

First and foremost, a healthy work/life balance enhances overall well-being. When employees can allocate sufficient time to their personal lives, they experience reduced stress and improved mental health. This, in turn, positively impacts their physical health, leading to increased energy levels and productivity. By taking time to relax, pursue hobbies, and spend quality time with loved ones, employees can recharge and maintain a positive mindset, making them more engaged and motivated at work.

Another significant benefit is increased job satisfaction. When employees have the opportunity to achieve a balance between their professional and personal obligations, they feel a greater sense of fulfillment in their roles. This satisfaction stems from the ability to pursue personal interests and achieve personal goals, leading to a more fulfilling and meaningful life.

Moreover, a work/life balance supports career growth and development. When employees have time for personal growth activities, such as attending training programs, pursuing higher education, or engaging in networking opportunities, they expand their knowledge and skills, making them more valuable assets to their employers. A well-rounded employee who has diverse experiences outside of work can bring fresh perspectives and innovative ideas to their professional roles.

Additionally, a healthy work/life balance fosters better relationships. When employees can prioritize their personal lives, they are more likely to build stronger connections with their families, friends, and communities. Strong personal relationships provide emotional support and a sense of belonging, which positively impacts an employee's overall happiness and satisfaction.

Lastly, a work/life balance promotes longevity and prevents burnout. When employees consistently prioritize work over personal needs, they risk experiencing burnout, which can lead to physical and mental health issues. By maintaining a balance, employees can preserve their health and well-being, ensuring long-term career success and fulfillment.

In conclusion, the benefits of a work/life balance for employees are vast. From improved well-being and job satisfaction to enhanced career growth and stronger relationships, finding equilibrium between work and personal life is crucial. Employers should recognize and support their employees in achieving this balance, as it not only benefits individuals but also contributes to a more productive and harmonious work environment.

The Role of Employers in Promoting Work/Life Balance

Introduction:
In today's fast-paced and demanding work environment, maintaining a healthy work/life balance has become more crucial than ever. As employees, we often find ourselves juggling multiple responsibilities, striving to excel in our professional lives while also taking care of our personal well-being. This subchapter explores the significant role that employers play in promoting work/life balance and highlights the importance of finding equilibrium between work and personal life.

Creating a Supportive Culture: Employers have the power to shape the work environment and establish a supportive culture that values work/life balance. By fostering a culture where employees are encouraged to prioritize their well-being and personal commitments, employers can enhance job satisfaction, productivity, and overall employee happiness. This can be achieved by implementing flexible work arrangements, such as remote work options, flextime, compressed workweeks, or job sharing. These initiatives allow employees to better manage their personal and professional commitments, reducing stress and improving work/life balance.

Providing Resources and Benefits: Employers can also play a crucial role in promoting work/life balance by providing resources and benefits that support employees' well-being. This can range from offering wellness programs, gym memberships, or on-site childcare facilities to organizing stress management workshops or encouraging regular breaks and vacations. By investing in these resources, employers demonstrate their commitment to their employees' overall health and happiness, which can lead to increased job satisfaction and loyalty.

Open Communication:
Employers should foster open communication channels that allow employees to express their work/life balance needs and concerns without fear of retribution. Regular check-ins, team meetings, and performance evaluations should include discussions about work/life balance and ways to improve it. Employers can also encourage managers to lead by example, demonstrating their own commitment to work/life balance and encouraging their teams to follow suit.

Supporting Personal Growth:
Employers can support work/life balance by promoting personal growth opportunities. By providing access to training and development programs, employers empower employees to enhance their skills and knowledge, which can lead to more efficient work practices and reduced work hours. Supporting personal growth not only benefits employees but also helps employers create a workforce that is more adaptable and capable of handling challenges effectively.

Conclusion:
Work/life balance is vital for maintaining physical and mental well-being and ensuring long-term career satisfaction. Employers have a crucial role in promoting work/life balance by creating a supportive culture, offering resources and benefits, fostering open communication, and supporting personal growth. By acknowledging the importance of work/life balance and actively working towards its promotion, employers can create a healthier and more engaged workforce, resulting in increased productivity and overall job

satisfaction. As employees, it is essential for us to advocate for work/life balance and collaborate with our employers to create an environment that prioritizes our well-being both inside and outside of work.

Employer responsibility towards work/life balance

Introduction:
In today's fast-paced world, maintaining a healthy work/life balance has become increasingly crucial. Employers play a significant role in shaping this balance for their employees. Recognizing the importance of work/life balance, progressive organizations are taking steps to create supportive environments that prioritize their employees' well-being. This subchapter explores the employer's responsibility towards work/life balance and its impact on employees.

Creating a Supportive Environment:
Employers have a responsibility to foster a supportive environment that promotes a healthy work/life balance. This includes implementing policies and practices that enable employees to manage their personal and professional commitments effectively. Flexible work arrangements, such as telecommuting, flexitime, and compressed workweeks, are examples of initiatives that allow employees to balance their work and personal lives more effectively.

Promoting Employee Well-being:
Employers should prioritize employee well-being by providing resources and programs that support physical, mental, and emotional health. This can include wellness programs, access to counseling services, and promoting a healthy lifestyle through partnerships with gyms or fitness centers. By investing in their employees' well-being, employers can reduce stress levels, improve morale, and enhance overall productivity.

Encouraging Work/Life Boundaries:
Employers should emphasize the importance of setting boundaries between work and personal life. This can be achieved by discouraging after-hours work and promoting time-off policies that encourage employees to take breaks and vacations. Furthermore, employers can foster a culture that respects employees' personal time and encourages a healthy separation between work and personal commitments.

Flexible Leave Policies:
Employers should implement flexible leave policies that accommodate employees' personal needs. Maternity and paternity leave, compassionate leave for family emergencies, and sabbatical programs are examples of policies that demonstrate an employer's commitment to work/life balance. By providing these opportunities, employers enable employees to prioritize their personal lives when necessary, reducing stress and improving job satisfaction.

Benefits of a Healthy Work/Life Balance:
A healthy work/life balance has numerous benefits for employees. It enhances overall well-being, reduces stress levels, and improves mental health. Employees with a good work/life balance are more motivated, engaged, and productive. They experience less burnout and have higher job satisfaction, leading to increased loyalty and retention. Additionally, a healthy work/life balance allows employees to be more present and engaged in their personal lives, fostering stronger relationships and overall happiness.

Conclusion:
Employers have a significant responsibility towards their employees' work/life balance. By creating a supportive environment, promoting

employee well-being, encouraging boundaries, and implementing flexible leave policies, employers can contribute to their employees' overall happiness and success. It is essential for employees to be aware of their rights and advocate for a healthy work/life balance, as it ultimately leads to a more fulfilling and enriched life both inside and outside of work.

Why employers should prioritize work/life balance

In today's fast-paced and demanding work environment, it is crucial for employers to prioritize work/life balance. The importance of a healthy work/life balance cannot be overstated, as it has a profound impact on an employee's overall well-being, productivity, and job satisfaction. In this subchapter, we will delve into the reasons why employers should make work/life balance a top priority.

First and foremost, a healthy work/life balance is essential for maintaining good physical and mental health. When employees are constantly overwhelmed by work and have little time for personal activities, it can lead to stress, burnout, and even serious health issues. By prioritizing work/life balance, employers can help prevent these negative consequences and promote the well-being of their workforce.

Moreover, a healthy work/life balance has a direct impact on productivity and job performance. When employees are given the opportunity to recharge and engage in activities outside of work, they return to their jobs with renewed energy and focus. On the other hand, employees who are constantly overworked and have no time for personal pursuits are more likely to experience decreased motivation, creativity, and efficiency. By prioritizing work/life balance, employers can cultivate a more engaged and productive workforce.

Furthermore, placing a high value on work/life balance can significantly improve employee retention and recruitment efforts. In today's competitive job market, employees are actively seeking employers who understand the importance of balancing work and personal life. By providing flexible scheduling options, promoting a healthy work culture, and offering benefits that support work/life balance, employers can attract top talent and retain valuable employees.

Lastly, prioritizing work/life balance is simply the right thing to do. Employees are not just resources or machines; they are human beings with families, personal aspirations, and a need for a fulfilling life outside of work. By acknowledging and respecting this need, employers can create a positive and supportive work environment that fosters loyalty, trust, and a sense of belonging.

In conclusion, employers should prioritize work/life balance for the well-being of their employees, the productivity of the organization, and the overall success of their business. By recognizing the importance of a healthy work/life balance, employers can create a workplace that values the holistic needs of their employees, leading to improved job satisfaction, increased productivity, and better retention rates.

Chapter 2: Creating a Flexible Work Environment

Flexible Work Arrangements

In today's fast-paced and demanding work environment, achieving a healthy work/life balance has become increasingly important. Employers are recognizing the need for flexibility in work arrangements to help their employees maintain a sense of equilibrium between their personal and professional lives. This subchapter explores the significance of flexible work arrangements and how they can empower employees to lead fulfilling lives.

Flexible work arrangements refer to any modifications made to traditional work schedules and locations. These arrangements may include part-time work, job sharing, telecommuting, compressed workweeks, or flextime. By adopting these practices, employers acknowledge that employees have responsibilities and commitments beyond the workplace and that their well-being is crucial for overall productivity and job satisfaction.

One of the key benefits of flexible work arrangements is the ability to better manage personal and family obligations. With the flexibility to adjust their work hours or location, employees can attend to their children's needs, care for aging parents, or pursue personal interests without sacrificing their career aspirations. This balance fosters a sense of fulfillment and reduces stress, ultimately leading to increased motivation, engagement, and loyalty.

Moreover, flexible work arrangements also contribute to improved mental and physical health. By reducing commuting time and allowing employees to work from home, they can avoid the stress and exhaustion associated with long hours spent in traffic or public transportation. This newfound freedom enables individuals to make time for exercise, relaxation, and self-care, resulting in a healthier and more energized workforce.

Another advantage of flexible work arrangements is the potential for increased productivity and creativity. When employees are given the freedom to choose when and where they work, they are more likely to be motivated, focused, and innovative. By tailoring their work schedules to align with their peak productivity hours, individuals can optimize their performance and produce high-quality work.

However, it is important to note that flexible work arrangements require effective communication and collaboration. Employers and employees must establish clear expectations, maintain open lines of communication, and utilize technology to ensure seamless coordination. By embracing flexibility while maintaining accountability, the work environment becomes more harmonious and supportive.

In conclusion, flexible work arrangements play a pivotal role in promoting a healthy work/life balance. By recognizing the importance of employees' personal lives and providing them with the flexibility they need, employers empower individuals to lead fulfilling lives. These arrangements enhance mental and physical well-being, increase productivity and creativity, and contribute to a positive and supportive work environment. As employees, it is crucial to advocate for flexible work arrangements and actively seek opportunities that align with our own work/life balance goals.

Telecommuting and remote work options

Telecommuting and Remote Work Options: Balancing Work and Life

In today's fast-paced and interconnected world, achieving a healthy work/life balance has become increasingly vital. As employees, we often find ourselves caught in the never-ending cycle of long commutes, demanding work schedules, and limited time for personal pursuits. However, with the advent of telecommuting and remote work options, a transformative shift in the traditional work environment has emerged, offering incredible benefits for both employers and employees.

Telecommuting, also known as remote work, refers to the practice of working from a location other than the traditional office space. This flexible work arrangement allows employees to complete their tasks and responsibilities from the comfort of their own homes or any other suitable location. The advantages of telecommuting are numerous and can greatly contribute to achieving a healthy work/life balance.

First and foremost, telecommuting eliminates the time-consuming and often stressful daily commute. No longer will employees have to endure rush hour traffic or crowded public transportation, saving precious hours that can be spent on personal pursuits or simply relaxing. Additionally, this reduced commute time leads to lower stress levels, increased job satisfaction, and improved overall mental health.

Furthermore, telecommuting offers increased flexibility in managing personal and family responsibilities. By working remotely, employees can better accommodate family commitments, such as childcare responsibilities or caring for elderly parents. This newfound flexibility enables individuals to maintain a healthy work/life balance, reducing the guilt or stress associated with trying to juggle competing demands.

Remote work options also foster a sense of autonomy and empowerment. Employees are no longer constrained by the rigidity of a traditional office setting, allowing them to tailor their work environments to suit their individual preferences and needs. This can lead to increased productivity, creativity, and job satisfaction, as employees are able to work in an environment that best suits their work style.

However, it is important to note that telecommuting also comes with its own set of challenges. Effective communication and collaboration become crucial in ensuring a seamless workflow, and employees must maintain discipline and self-motivation to stay on track. Employers must establish clear guidelines and expectations to ensure accountability and maintain productivity within remote teams.

In conclusion, telecommuting and remote work options offer a transformative solution to achieving a healthy work/life balance. By eliminating the daily commute, providing increased flexibility, and fostering autonomy, these flexible work arrangements empower employees to take control of their lives while meeting their professional obligations. As employees, it is essential to explore and advocate for these options, as they have the potential to revolutionize the way we work and live. Let us embrace the power of flexibility and create a harmonious integration of work and life.

Flextime and compressed workweeks

Flextime and compressed workweeks: Finding the perfect work-life balance

In today's fast-paced and demanding work environment, achieving a healthy work-life balance has become more critical than ever. As employees, we often find ourselves struggling to juggle our personal and professional commitments, leading to stress, burnout, and diminished overall well-being. However, the concept of flextime and compressed workweeks offers a potential solution to this dilemma, enabling us to regain control over our time and find harmony between our work and personal lives.

Flextime, also known as flexible working hours, allows employees to have greater control over their daily work schedules. Instead of adhering to the traditional 9-to-5 routine, flextime enables individuals to determine when they start and finish their workday, within certain parameters set by the employer. This flexibility empowers employees to align their work hours with their personal obligations, such as attending family events, pursuing hobbies, or taking care of personal errands. By having the freedom to choose when they work, employees can better manage their time, reduce stress levels, and increase productivity.

Compressed workweeks, on the other hand, involve condensing the standard workweek into fewer but longer days. For instance, instead of working five eight-hour days, employees might work four ten-hour days. This arrangement allows individuals to enjoy longer weekends, providing them with more quality time to recharge, spend with loved ones, or pursue personal interests. By compressing their workweek, employees can experience increased job satisfaction, reduced commuting time, and improved work-life integration.

The benefits of flextime and compressed workweeks extend beyond personal well-being. Employers who embrace these practices often witness a positive impact on productivity, employee morale, and retention rates. By acknowledging the importance of work-life balance, employers demonstrate their commitment to the overall well-being of their workforce, leading to a more engaged and motivated team. Additionally, flextime and compressed workweeks can also contribute to a more diverse and inclusive workplace, as they accommodate the needs of individuals with different responsibilities and lifestyles.

In conclusion, flextime and compressed workweeks serve as powerful tools in achieving a healthy work-life balance. As employees, it is essential to communicate our needs and explore these options with our employers. By finding a balance between our professional and personal lives, we can enhance our overall well-being, improve job satisfaction, and cultivate a more fulfilling and harmonious lifestyle.

Benefits of Flexibility for Employees

In today's fast-paced and demanding work environment, finding a healthy work/life balance has become increasingly important. As employees strive to meet their professional goals while also maintaining a fulfilling personal life, flexibility in the workplace has emerged as a valuable solution. This subchapter explores the numerous benefits that flexibility offers to employees, ultimately highlighting the significance of a healthy work/life balance.

First and foremost, flexibility allows employees to have greater control over their schedules. Traditional 9-to-5 jobs often restrict individuals, leaving little room for personal commitments or unexpected events. However, with flexible work arrangements, employees can adapt their work hours to accommodate family responsibilities, personal interests, or even pursue further education. This newfound control empowers individuals to make the most of their time and achieve a better balance between their personal and professional lives.

Moreover, flexibility in the workplace has been proven to reduce stress levels among employees. Juggling multiple responsibilities can easily lead to burnout and decreased productivity. By introducing flexibility, employers provide their workforce with the opportunity to manage their workload in a way that aligns with their individual needs and preferences. As a result, employees can better prioritize their tasks, leading to increased job satisfaction and reduced stress levels. This, in turn, fosters a healthier work environment and enhances overall employee well-being.

Additionally, flexibility promotes a higher sense of loyalty and commitment among employees. When employers acknowledge and accommodate the personal needs and aspirations of their workforce, a culture of trust and appreciation is cultivated. Employees who feel supported in achieving a work/life balance are more likely to remain loyal to their organization and go the extra mile to contribute to its success. This increased loyalty not only benefits the employee but also enhances the overall performance and productivity of the company.

In conclusion, the benefits of flexibility for employees are far-reaching and essential in maintaining a healthy work/life balance. By providing greater control over schedules, reducing stress levels, and fostering loyalty, flexibility in the workplace enables employees to lead more fulfilling lives both personally and professionally. Employers who recognize the importance of work/life balance and offer flexible arrangements ultimately create a positive and supportive environment that benefits everyone involved.

Increased productivity and job satisfaction

In today's fast-paced and competitive work environment, the importance of a healthy work/life balance cannot be overstated. The demands of our professional lives often spill over into our personal lives, causing stress, burnout, and a general sense of dissatisfaction. However, employers are increasingly recognizing the value of promoting work/life balance, not only for the well-being of their employees but also for the overall success of their organizations.

One of the key benefits of achieving a healthy work/life balance is increased productivity. When employees are well-rested, mentally and physically, they are more focused and motivated to perform their tasks efficiently. Research has consistently shown that individuals who feel balanced and fulfilled in their personal lives are more engaged and productive at work. By allowing time for personal activities, such as exercise, hobbies, and spending time with loved ones, employees can recharge their batteries, resulting in higher levels of productivity during working hours.

Furthermore, a healthy work/life balance leads to greater job satisfaction. When employees feel they have enough time for both their professional and personal lives, they experience a sense of fulfillment and contentment. This, in turn, fosters a positive work environment, with employees who are more committed to their roles and the success of the organization. Job satisfaction also translates into increased loyalty, reduced turnover, and improved employee retention rates, which are all crucial factors for a company's long-term success.

Employers can play a vital role in promoting work/life balance among their workforce. By implementing flexible working arrangements, such as remote work options, flexible hours, and compressed workweeks, employers can empower employees to better manage their personal responsibilities while meeting their professional obligations. Additionally, providing support programs, such as employee assistance programs, wellness initiatives, and work/life balance training, can further enhance employee well-being and job satisfaction.

In conclusion, finding a healthy work/life balance is essential for both employees and employers. By promoting work/life balance, employers can unlock the potential for increased productivity and job satisfaction among their workforce. Employees who feel supported in managing their personal and professional lives are more likely to be engaged, productive, and loyal, ultimately contributing to the overall success of the organization. It is crucial for employees to prioritize their well-being and communicate their needs to their employers, fostering a culture that values work/life balance and reaps the benefits of a happier and more fulfilled workforce.

Better work/life integration

Subchapter: Better Work/Life Integration

In today's fast-paced and demanding world, achieving a healthy work/life balance has become more challenging than ever before. As employees, we often find ourselves juggling multiple responsibilities, struggling to find time for ourselves, our families, and our personal pursuits. However, the key to finding fulfillment lies in achieving a better work/life integration.

Work/life integration focuses on creating harmony between our professional and personal lives, rather than viewing them as separate entities. It emphasizes the importance of finding a synergy that allows us to excel in both aspects, leading to increased productivity, satisfaction, and overall well-being.

One crucial aspect of better work/life integration is recognizing the significance of a healthy work/life balance. It is essential to acknowledge that our personal lives are just as important as our professional commitments. By prioritizing our well-being and nurturing our relationships outside of work, we can bring a sense of fulfillment and happiness to both spheres of our lives.

Achieving a better work/life integration requires a proactive approach. It involves setting clear boundaries and effectively managing our time and energy. Employers play a critical role in shaping the work/life balance of their employees. Forward-thinking organizations understand that a flexible work environment can significantly contribute to better integration.

Flexible work arrangements, such as remote work, flextime, or compressed workweeks, can empower employees to have more control over their schedules and allow them to fulfill personal responsibilities without sacrificing their professional commitments. Such arrangements enable employees to attend to family needs, pursue personal interests, or maintain a healthy lifestyle, ultimately leading to increased job satisfaction and loyalty.

Furthermore, organizations that prioritize work/life integration often encourage open communication and support networks among employees. By fostering a culture of understanding and empathy, employers can create an environment where individuals feel comfortable discussing their work/life challenges and seeking support from their peers and superiors.

In conclusion, better work/life integration is crucial for employees seeking a fulfilling and balanced life. By recognizing the importance of a healthy work/life balance and adopting flexible work arrangements, employers can empower their workforce to excel in both personal and professional domains. It is through this integration that we can find true happiness, productivity, and overall satisfaction in our lives. Remember, it's not about separating work from life but rather integrating the two harmoniously.

Chapter 3: Flexible Leave Options

Paid Time Off (PTO) Policies

In today's fast-paced world, achieving a healthy work/life balance can seem like an elusive goal. The demands of our professional lives often leave little time for personal pursuits and self-care. However, employers are increasingly recognizing the importance of supporting their employees' well-being, both inside and outside the workplace. One way companies are addressing this crucial need is through the implementation of Paid Time Off (PTO) policies.

PTO policies offer employees the opportunity to take time away from work for personal reasons, without sacrificing their pay. These policies typically encompass various types of leave, such as vacation days, personal days, and sick leave, allowing individuals to attend to their physical and mental health, spend quality time with loved ones, and pursue personal interests.

One of the primary benefits of PTO policies is that they enable employees to recharge and rejuvenate. Taking regular breaks from work helps prevent burnout, increases productivity, and enhances overall job satisfaction. By offering PTO, employers acknowledge the importance of self-care and recognize that employees who are well-rested and emotionally fulfilled perform better in their roles.

Moreover, PTO policies promote a healthy work/life balance. They send a powerful message that work is not the only aspect of an individual's life, and that personal commitments and interests deserve equal attention. By allowing employees to take time off when needed, employers demonstrate their commitment to supporting their staff's happiness and well-being. This, in turn, fosters loyalty, boosts morale, and contributes to a positive work environment.

Another advantage of PTO policies is that they provide flexibility. Rather than segregating time off into specific categories like vacation or sick leave, employees can use their PTO days as they see fit. This flexibility allows individuals to tailor their time off to their unique circumstances, whether they need a mental health day, an extended vacation, or time to attend to personal matters. By granting this flexibility, employers demonstrate trust in their employees' judgment and promote a culture of autonomy and respect.

It is important for employees to familiarize themselves with their organization's specific PTO policies. Understanding the guidelines and procedures helps individuals plan their time off effectively and ensures a smooth process for requesting and receiving approval for leave. Additionally, employees should be aware of any limitations or restrictions to ensure they comply with their employer's expectations.

In conclusion, PTO policies play a crucial role in promoting a healthy work/life balance. By offering employees the opportunity to take time off for personal reasons, employers demonstrate their commitment to their staff's well-being and foster a positive work environment. PTO policies provide employees with the flexibility they need to address personal commitments and interests, while also promoting rest and rejuvenation. It is essential for employees to familiarize themselves with their organization's specific PTO policies to make the most of this valuable benefit. Remember, taking care of yourself is just as important as excelling in your professional life, and PTO policies can help you achieve that delicate balance.

Different types of PTO policies

In today's fast-paced and demanding work environment, achieving a healthy work/life balance has become increasingly important. Employers are recognizing the significance of supporting their employees' well-being, leading to the implementation of various policies, including Paid Time Off (PTO) policies. In this subchapter, we will explore the different types of PTO policies that employers may offer to promote a healthy work/life balance.

1. Traditional PTO: This is the most common type of PTO policy, where employees accrue a set number of hours or days off based on their length of service. Whether it is sick leave, vacation time, or personal days, employees can utilize this time as needed, allowing them to recharge and address personal matters without the fear of losing income.

2. Unlimited PTO: Some forward-thinking companies have adopted unlimited PTO policies, which give employees the freedom to take time off as they need without a predetermined limit. This policy encourages a culture of trust and flexibility, empowering employees to manage their time effectively and prioritize their personal well-being.

3. Floating Holidays: This type of PTO policy offers employees a set number of days off that they can use for specific holidays of their choice. By recognizing that individuals may celebrate different holidays or have cultural observances, floating holidays allow employees to align their time off with their personal needs and values.

4. Family-Friendly PTO: Recognizing the importance of family, some employers offer specific PTO policies that cater to employees with

dependents. This may include additional parental leave, flexible scheduling, or the option to work remotely. Such policies acknowledge the challenges of balancing work and family life and provide support to employees in their caregiving responsibilities.

5. Volunteering Time Off (VTO): In line with corporate social responsibility initiatives, some employers provide employees with dedicated time off to engage in community service or volunteer activities. VTO policies not only contribute to employee satisfaction but also promote a sense of purpose and social impact.

It is important for employees to be aware of the various PTO policies available in their organizations. Understanding the options and benefits associated with each type of policy empowers individuals to make informed decisions and take advantage of the opportunities provided to achieve a healthy work/life balance.

In conclusion, PTO policies play a significant role in supporting and promoting a healthy work/life balance. From traditional to unlimited PTO, floating holidays to family-friendly policies, and volunteering time off, employers are actively working towards creating a more flexible and supportive work environment. By embracing these policies, employees can prioritize their well-being, improve job satisfaction, and ultimately lead more fulfilling lives both inside and outside of work.

Guidelines for requesting and utilizing PTO

In today's fast-paced and demanding work environment, maintaining a healthy work/life balance is more important than ever. Striking a harmonious equilibrium between your professional and personal lives is crucial for your overall well-being and productivity. One valuable tool that can aid in achieving this balance is Paid Time Off (PTO). This subchapter aims to provide employees with essential guidelines for requesting and utilizing PTO effectively.

First and foremost, it is essential to understand the purpose of PTO. This benefit is designed to grant employees a designated amount of time off, with full or partial pay, for personal reasons such as vacation, illness, or family commitments. Recognizing the significance of PTO is the first step in utilizing it wisely.

To make the most of your PTO, it is important to plan ahead. Consider the duration and timing of your absence to ensure minimal disruption to your team and work processes. Communicate your intentions well in advance, allowing your supervisor and colleagues ample time to adjust schedules and delegate tasks. By planning ahead, you can minimize stress and ensure a smooth workflow during your absence.

When requesting PTO, be sure to follow your company's specific policies and procedures. Familiarize yourself with the guidelines outlined in your employee handbook or policy manual to ensure compliance. These guidelines may include notifying your supervisor or Human Resources department in writing, using a designated time-off request form, or adhering to specific blackout periods when PTO is not permitted.

Additionally, consider the needs of your team and organization before requesting PTO. If certain periods are particularly busy or critical for your department, it may be more appropriate to postpone your time off. Being mindful of the workload and dependencies of others demonstrates a commitment to teamwork and the success of your organization.

Lastly, while on PTO, truly disconnect from work. Resist the temptation to check emails or respond to work-related calls. Use this time to recharge, relax, and focus on your personal well-being. Engage in activities that bring you joy, spend quality time with loved ones, or explore new hobbies. Remember, the purpose of PTO is to rejuvenate and return to work with renewed energy and focus.

In conclusion, utilizing PTO effectively is essential for maintaining a healthy work/life balance. By following these guidelines, you can ensure a seamless process for requesting and utilizing your time off. Remember, PTO is not just a benefit but a necessary tool for personal well-being and professional success.

Parental Leave Policies

In today's fast-paced world, achieving a healthy work/life balance has become more important than ever. As employees, we strive to excel in our careers while also maintaining fulfilling personal lives. One crucial aspect of achieving this balance is having access to adequate parental leave policies.

Parental leave policies are designed to support employees who are starting or expanding their families. These policies recognize the importance of bonding with a new child, adjusting to the demands of parenthood, and ensuring the well-being of both the parent and the child. They provide employees with the time and space to transition smoothly into their new roles as parents, without sacrificing their professional growth.

A progressive and forward-thinking employer understands that investing in parental leave policies is not only beneficial for employees but also for the organization as a whole. By offering generous parental leave, employers demonstrate their commitment to supporting their employees' personal lives and well-being. This, in turn, fosters loyalty, enhances employee morale, and boosts productivity. Employees who feel valued and supported are more likely to be engaged, motivated, and focused on their work, resulting in higher job satisfaction and lower turnover rates.

Moreover, parental leave policies have broader societal benefits. They contribute to gender equality by enabling both mothers and fathers to take time off and share caregiving responsibilities. This helps break down traditional gender roles and promotes a more balanced distribution of domestic duties. In addition, parental leave policies have been shown to have positive effects on the physical and mental health of parents, which, in turn, benefits the overall well-being of families and communities.

As employees, it is essential for us to be aware of our rights and benefits regarding parental leave. By understanding the policies offered by our employers, we can make informed decisions about our personal and professional lives. We should seek out organizations that prioritize work/life balance and offer generous parental leave policies. Additionally, we should advocate for improved parental leave policies at both the organizational and societal levels, recognizing the importance of this issue for all employees.

In conclusion, parental leave policies play a vital role in achieving a healthy work/life balance. They benefit employees, employers, and society as a whole. By valuing and supporting employees during this critical phase of their lives, employers can create a workplace culture that promotes flexibility and well-being. As employees, let us be proactive in understanding and advocating for parental leave policies that reflect our needs and aspirations. Together, we can shape a future where work and personal life harmoniously coexist.

Maternity and paternity leave options

In today's modern world, the importance of a healthy work-life balance cannot be overstated. As employees, we understand the demands of our professional lives, but it is equally vital to prioritize our personal lives, especially when it comes to starting and nurturing a family. Recognizing this need, many employers have embraced the concept of maternity and paternity leave, providing a supportive and flexible environment for employees during this special time.

Maternity leave is a crucial benefit that allows expectant mothers to take time off from work before and after childbirth. It not only provides the necessary physical recovery time but also creates an opportunity for new mothers to bond with their newborns. This period of leave typically varies from company to company, but it often ranges from six to twelve weeks. During maternity leave, employees are entitled to job protection, ensuring they can return to their position or an equivalent one once their leave is over.

Similarly, paternity leave is designed to support new fathers in their transition into parenthood. It recognizes the importance of their involvement in their child's early development and allows them to take time off work to care for and bond with their newborn. While the duration of paternity leave may vary, it is becoming increasingly common for employers to offer several weeks of leave to new fathers.

Furthermore, some progressive companies have gone beyond the traditional maternity and paternity leave policies by introducing innovative options such as shared parental leave. This approach allows both parents to divide the leave period between them, giving them the flexibility to decide who will take time off and when. Shared parental leave promotes gender equality, encourages active involvement of both parents in childcare responsibilities, and enables a smoother transition back to work for both individuals.

Employers who prioritize the well-being of their employees understand that supporting their journey into parenthood is not only a moral imperative but also a business advantage. By offering maternity and paternity leave options, companies foster a positive work environment that attracts and retains top talent. Moreover, such policies result in increased employee loyalty, motivation, and productivity, as employees feel valued and supported by their organization.

In conclusion, maternity and paternity leave options play a vital role in promoting a healthy work-life balance for employees. Whether it's providing new mothers with the necessary time to recover and bond with their newborns or allowing fathers to actively participate in their child's early development, these policies demonstrate an employer's commitment to supporting their employees' personal lives. By embracing the power of flexibility, companies can create an environment that nurtures and supports their employees, ultimately leading to happier and more productive teams.

Supporting new parents in the workplace

As an employee, it is important to recognize the significance of a healthy work/life balance, especially when it comes to new parents in the workplace. The transition to parenthood is an incredible milestone, but it can also bring about a multitude of challenges. Employers have a crucial role to play in ensuring that new parents feel supported during this transformative phase of their lives.

First and foremost, it is vital for employers to create a nurturing and inclusive work environment that acknowledges the needs and responsibilities of new parents. This can be achieved by implementing policies that allow for flexible work arrangements, such as remote work options, flexible hours, and compressed workweeks. By offering these flexible options, employers can empower new parents to better manage their work and family obligations, ultimately enhancing their overall well-being.

Another essential aspect of supporting new parents is providing comprehensive parental leave policies. Paid parental leave allows new parents to take time off to care for their newborns without worrying about their financial stability. This period of bonding and adjustment is critical for both parents and children, and employers should recognize the importance of offering generous and inclusive parental leave policies.

Furthermore, employers can establish employee resource groups or support networks specifically tailored to new parents. These groups can provide a platform for sharing experiences, advice, and resources, fostering a sense of community and understanding among employees who are going through similar situations. By facilitating an open and supportive environment, employers can help alleviate the stress and isolation often experienced by new parents.

Additionally, employers can offer on-site amenities such as childcare facilities or partnerships with local daycare centers. This not only addresses the practical need for childcare but also demonstrates a commitment to supporting new parents and their families. By providing these services, employers can alleviate the burden on new parents, allowing them to focus on their work knowing their children are well cared for.

In conclusion, supporting new parents in the workplace is crucial for maintaining a healthy work/life balance. Employers can achieve this by implementing flexible work arrangements, offering comprehensive parental leave policies, establishing support networks, and providing on-site childcare options. By prioritizing the needs of new parents, employers can create a positive and inclusive work culture that values the well-being of their employees and their families.

Chapter 4: Supporting Employee Well-being

Wellness Programs

Wellness Programs: Promoting a Healthy Work/Life Balance

In today's fast-paced and demanding work environment, achieving a healthy work/life balance has become more crucial than ever. With mounting stress levels and diminishing personal time, many employees find it challenging to prioritize their well-being. Recognizing this predicament, forward-thinking organizations have begun implementing wellness programs aimed at promoting a healthier and more balanced lifestyle. This subchapter explores the significance of wellness programs and their impact on employees' work/life balance.

A healthy work/life balance is vital for overall well-being, both personally and professionally. It serves as a foundation for individuals to lead fulfilling lives, fostering happiness, productivity, and job satisfaction. Wellness programs play a pivotal role in helping employees strike this delicate equilibrium by providing resources and support to enhance their physical and mental well-being.

One of the primary benefits of wellness programs is their ability to alleviate stress. Work-related stress is a prevalent issue that adversely affects employees' health and performance. Wellness initiatives such as stress management workshops, meditation sessions, and yoga classes equip employees with effective coping mechanisms to manage stress effectively. By reducing stress levels, employees can achieve better work/life balance, enhance their productivity, and maintain a positive mindset.

Furthermore, these programs offer various avenues for improving physical health. Regular exercise, nutrition counseling, and access to fitness facilities are often included in wellness programs. Encouraging employees to adopt healthy habits and providing them with the necessary tools not only improves their physical health but also boosts their energy levels and overall performance. By prioritizing their well-being, employees can bring their best selves to work and achieve greater job satisfaction.

Wellness programs also address the mental well-being of employees. Mental health challenges are increasingly prevalent in today's society, and the workplace is no exception. Offering resources such as counseling services, mental health awareness campaigns, and workshops on stress management and resilience equips employees with the necessary tools to navigate personal and professional challenges with greater ease. By addressing mental health concerns, organizations demonstrate their commitment to employee well-being, fostering a supportive and inclusive work environment.

In conclusion, wellness programs are invaluable in fostering a healthy work/life balance for employees. By prioritizing well-being, organizations recognize the importance of nurturing their most valuable asset – their workforce. These programs not only alleviate stress, but also enhance physical and mental health, leading to increased productivity, job satisfaction, and overall happiness. It is essential for employees to take advantage of the resources and support offered by wellness programs to achieve a harmonious work/life balance and lead a fulfilling life.

Health and fitness initiatives

In today's fast-paced and demanding work environment, maintaining a healthy work/life balance has become more crucial than ever. It is no secret that the daily grind can take a toll on our physical and mental well-being. That's why it is imperative for employees to prioritize their health and fitness, and for employers to support them in achieving a healthy work/life balance. This subchapter will explore the significance of health and fitness initiatives and the positive impact they can have on employees' overall well-being.

Recognizing the importance of a healthy work/life balance, employers have increasingly adopted health and fitness initiatives to promote employee wellness. These initiatives encompass a wide range of activities and programs designed to improve physical fitness, mental health, and overall quality of life. From on-site gyms and fitness classes to wellness programs and employee assistance programs, employers are stepping up their efforts to ensure their employees have access to resources that promote a healthy lifestyle.

One of the key benefits of health and fitness initiatives is the positive impact they have on employees' physical health. Encouraging regular exercise and providing fitness facilities at the workplace not only helps employees stay fit but also reduces the risk of chronic illnesses such as heart disease, obesity, and diabetes. By investing in the health of their workforce, employers not only improve productivity but also reduce healthcare costs in the long run.

In addition to physical health, mental well-being plays a significant role in maintaining a healthy work/life balance. Stress, anxiety, and burnout are common challenges faced by employees today. Health and fitness initiatives can help alleviate these issues by providing stress management programs, mindfulness training, and access to mental health resources. By addressing these concerns, employers create a supportive and nurturing environment that allows employees to thrive both personally and professionally.

Furthermore, health and fitness initiatives contribute to a positive work culture. When employees feel supported in their pursuit of a healthy lifestyle, they are more likely to feel valued and satisfied in their jobs. This, in turn, leads to increased engagement and productivity. Additionally, these initiatives foster camaraderie and teamwork among employees, as they participate in group fitness activities or wellness challenges together.

In conclusion, health and fitness initiatives are essential for maintaining a healthy work/life balance. By investing in employee wellness, employers not only improve physical and mental health but also create a positive work culture. These initiatives contribute to increased productivity, reduced healthcare costs, and overall job satisfaction. As employees, it is crucial to take advantage of these initiatives and prioritize our health and well-being, as they are integral to leading a fulfilling and balanced life.

Mental health support and resources

In today's fast-paced and demanding work environment, maintaining a healthy work/life balance is crucial for our overall well-being. As employees, we often find ourselves juggling multiple responsibilities, both in our professional and personal lives. However, neglecting our mental health can have long-term consequences on our performance, relationships, and overall happiness. That's why it is essential to recognize the importance of mental health support and the available resources that can help us navigate the challenges we face.

1. Understanding the Impact: Mental health is not something to be taken lightly. The stress and pressure of work can lead to burnout, anxiety, depression, and other mental health issues. Recognizing the signs and understanding the impact these conditions can have on our lives is the first step towards seeking help.

2. Encouraging Open Conversations: Creating a supportive and inclusive work environment starts with open conversations about mental health. Employers can play a significant role in reducing the stigma surrounding mental health by promoting dialogue and offering platforms for employees to share their experiences.

3. Employee Assistance Programs (EAP): Many organizations provide Employee Assistance Programs to support their employees' mental health needs. These programs often offer confidential counseling services, resources for stress management, and tools to enhance emotional well-being. Familiarize yourself with the EAP available in your workplace and take advantage of the services they offer.

4. Mental Health Awareness Campaigns: Companies are increasingly recognizing the importance of mental health and organizing awareness campaigns to educate employees about available resources and destigmatize seeking help. Stay informed about such initiatives and actively participate to enhance your knowledge and understanding of mental health issues.

5. Self-Care Practices: Alongside external support, it is crucial to develop self-care practices that promote mental well-being. Prioritize activities that help you relax and unwind, such as exercise, mindfulness, hobbies, and spending quality time with loved ones. Remember, self-care is not selfish; it is essential for maintaining a healthy work/life balance.

6. Building a Support Network: Surrounding yourself with a supportive network of colleagues, friends, and family members can make a significant difference in your mental health journey. Reach out to those you trust and share your challenges, as they may offer valuable insights or simply lend an empathetic ear.

Remember, mental health is a journey, and seeking support is a sign of strength, not weakness. By prioritizing your mental well-being and utilizing the resources available to you, you can better navigate the demands of work and life, leading to a more fulfilling and balanced existence.

Work/Life Integration Support

In today's fast-paced and demanding world, achieving a healthy work/life balance has become an essential goal for employees. The concept of work/life integration offers a fresh perspective, recognizing that work and personal life are not separate entities but rather interconnected parts of our overall well-being. To help you navigate this delicate balance, employers are now offering various forms of work/life integration support.

The importance of a healthy work/life balance cannot be overstated. It is crucial for your mental, physical, and emotional well-being. When work overwhelms your personal life, stress levels rise, and burnout becomes a real risk. On the other hand, neglecting work responsibilities for personal matters can lead to a lack of career progression and financial stability. Striking a harmonious integration between work and personal life is thus essential for overall satisfaction and success.

Recognizing this need, organizations have begun to provide valuable resources to support their employees' work/life integration. These initiatives aim to enhance employee well-being and productivity, fostering an environment where individuals feel supported and empowered to manage their professional and personal responsibilities effectively.

One form of work/life integration support is flexible working arrangements. Employers now offer options like telecommuting, compressed workweeks, and flexible hours to accommodate personal needs without compromising work performance. These arrangements allow you to attend to personal obligations while still meeting work deadlines and contributing to the team's success.

Additionally, companies are investing in employee assistance programs (EAPs) and wellness initiatives. EAPs provide confidential counseling services and support for personal and work-related challenges, ensuring employees have access to the help they need. Wellness programs promote physical and mental health through initiatives such as gym memberships, stress management workshops, and mindfulness training. These initiatives encourage self-care and provide essential tools for maintaining a healthy work/life integration.

Moreover, organizations are fostering a culture that values work/life integration. By encouraging open communication and setting realistic expectations, employers create an environment where employees feel comfortable discussing their personal needs. This culture shift helps reduce guilt or fear associated with balancing work and personal life and promotes a supportive and understanding workplace.

In conclusion, work/life integration support is becoming increasingly important in today's work environment. Employers are recognizing the significance of a healthy work/life balance and offering various resources to help employees achieve this integration. By embracing flexible working arrangements, implementing EAPs and wellness initiatives, and fostering a supportive culture, companies are empowering their employees to manage their professional and personal responsibilities effectively. Remember, a healthy work/life integration is not only crucial for your well-being but also enhances productivity and overall job satisfaction.

Childcare and eldercare assistance

Childcare and Eldercare Assistance: Balancing Work and Family Responsibilities

In today's fast-paced and demanding work environment, maintaining a healthy work-life balance has become increasingly crucial for employees. As the demands of work continue to increase, so does the need for reliable and effective childcare and eldercare assistance. Recognizing the importance of supporting employees in managing their family responsibilities, many employers are now offering innovative solutions to help employees strike a balance between their personal and professional lives.

Childcare and eldercare assistance programs have emerged as powerful tools for employers to support their workforce. By acknowledging the unique challenges faced by employees in juggling work and family commitments, these programs aim to alleviate the stress and worry associated with finding suitable care arrangements for loved ones. Whether it's providing access to affordable and quality childcare centers or offering flexible work hours to accommodate caregiving responsibilities, employers can play a pivotal role in fostering a healthy work-life balance for their employees.

For working parents, reliable and affordable childcare options are paramount. Many employers now offer on-site childcare facilities or partner with local daycare centers to provide employees with convenient and high-quality care for their children. This not only gives parents peace of mind but also allows them to focus on their work without worrying about their children's wellbeing. Moreover, some companies offer financial assistance, such as subsidies or flexible spending accounts, to help ease the financial burden of childcare expenses.

Similarly, as the population ages, eldercare has become a pressing concern for many employees. Employers are increasingly recognizing the importance of supporting employees who may have aging parents or other elderly dependents. Some companies offer resources and referrals to help employees find suitable eldercare providers, while others provide flexible work arrangements, such as telecommuting or flexible schedules, to enable employees to care for their elderly loved ones.

By prioritizing and investing in childcare and eldercare assistance programs, employers not only demonstrate their commitment to their employees' well-being but also reap the benefits of a more engaged and productive workforce. Employees who have access to reliable and supportive childcare and eldercare assistance are more likely to experience reduced stress levels and increased job satisfaction, which in turn can lead to higher retention rates and improved productivity.

In conclusion, recognizing the importance of a healthy work-life balance, employers are increasingly offering childcare and eldercare assistance programs to support their employees. By providing access to affordable and high-quality care options, employers empower employees to fulfill their family responsibilities without compromising their professional obligations. These programs are not only a testament to an employer's commitment to their workforce but also contribute to a more engaged and productive work environment. Ultimately, by embracing the power of flexibility and supporting employees' work-life balance, employers can create a win-win situation that benefits both the employees and the organization as a whole.

Flexible scheduling during personal emergencies

Life is unpredictable, and personal emergencies can arise when we least expect them. Whether it's a sudden illness, a family emergency, or a personal crisis, these situations can throw our lives into disarray and make it challenging to balance our personal responsibilities with our work commitments. Recognizing the importance of a healthy work/life balance, employers now offer flexible scheduling options to support their employees during personal emergencies.

Flexible scheduling during personal emergencies provides employees with the opportunity to manage their personal challenges while fulfilling their work obligations. This subchapter aims to shed light on the benefits of flexible scheduling and how employees can effectively navigate these situations.

First and foremost, flexible scheduling allows employees to address their personal emergencies without the added stress of worrying about work. This means having the freedom to adjust their work hours, work remotely, or take time off as needed. By understanding the importance of a healthy work/life balance, employers empower their employees to prioritize their well-being and that of their loved ones.

Having the ability to modify work schedules during personal emergencies also fosters loyalty and trust between employers and employees. When employees feel supported and understood during challenging times, they are more likely to remain committed and engaged with their work. This mutually beneficial relationship creates a positive work environment that values the personal needs of employees.

To effectively navigate personal emergencies, employees must proactively communicate with their employers. This subchapter will provide guidance on how to have open and honest conversations about personal emergencies, ensuring that employers are aware of the situation and can assist in finding the best solution. It will also cover the importance of planning ahead, setting clear expectations, and maintaining transparent communication throughout the process.

In conclusion, flexible scheduling during personal emergencies is a vital component of a healthy work/life balance. Employers who understand its significance empower their employees to prioritize their personal well-being while fulfilling their work obligations. By providing flexibility, employers foster trust, loyalty, and commitment among their workforce. In this subchapter, employees will gain valuable insights on effectively navigating personal emergencies, including how to communicate with employers and plan ahead. Remember, your well-being matters, and employers who embrace flexibility during personal emergencies are invested in your success both personally and professionally.

In today's fast-paced world, achieving a healthy work/life balance has become increasingly essential. We are constantly juggling various responsibilities, including work, family, and personal obligations. Unfortunately, personal emergencies can arise unexpectedly, disrupting our carefully planned schedules. However, with the power of flexibility, employers can help employees navigate these challenging situations more effectively.

The subchapter "Flexible Scheduling During Personal Emergencies" explores the importance of accommodating employees during times of crisis. It delves into how employers can create a supportive environment that allows individuals to address personal emergencies without compromising their work commitments.

One of the key aspects of flexible scheduling during personal emergencies is understanding that unexpected situations can arise at any time. Whether it's a family member falling ill, a car accident, or any other crisis, employees need the flexibility to handle these situations promptly. Employers can play a crucial role by offering flexible working hours, remote work options, or allowing employees to use their vacation or personal days as needed. By providing these options, employers ensure that employees can attend to their personal emergencies without fear of negative consequences.

Additionally, effective communication is vital during times of personal emergencies. Employers should encourage open and honest conversations, allowing employees to communicate their needs and concerns. This open dialogue fosters understanding and enables employers to provide the necessary support and flexibility.

Furthermore, employers can consider implementing policies that offer paid or unpaid leave specifically for personal emergencies. This not only demonstrates a commitment to employees' well-being but also helps alleviate the financial stress that often accompanies personal crises.

By prioritizing flexible scheduling during personal emergencies, employers show their dedication to a healthy work/life balance. This approach not only enhances employee satisfaction and loyalty but also fosters a positive work environment. Employees can rest assured that their personal emergencies will be handled with care and understanding, creating a sense of security and trust within the organization.

In conclusion, the subchapter "Flexible Scheduling During Personal Emergencies" emphasizes the importance of accommodating employees during times of crisis. Employers who prioritize flexibility and understanding in such situations create a supportive work environment that values work/life balance. By implementing policies such as flexible working hours, remote work options, and leave policies, employers can assist employees in navigating personal emergencies while maintaining their professional commitments. Together, employers and employees can create a harmonious work environment that acknowledges and supports the challenges individuals face outside of the workplace.

Chapter 5: Promoting Work/Life Balance Culture

Leadership and Management Support

Leadership and Management Support: Empowering Employees for a Healthy Work/Life Balance

In today's fast-paced and demanding work environment, achieving a healthy work/life balance has become an essential goal for employees. As individuals strive to find harmony between their personal and professional lives, it is crucial for organizations to recognize the importance of providing leadership and management support in this endeavor.

Leadership plays a pivotal role in shaping the work culture and setting the tone for work/life balance. When leaders actively promote and support a healthy balance, employees feel empowered to prioritize their personal commitments without compromising their professional responsibilities. They understand that their well-being matters and that the organization values their overall happiness and satisfaction.

Management support is equally vital in creating an environment that fosters work/life balance. Managers who are attentive, understanding, and flexible in accommodating their employees' personal needs build trust and loyalty. By offering flexible work arrangements, such as telecommuting or flexible scheduling, managers demonstrate their commitment to supporting their team members' well-being. This support not only enhances employee morale but also boosts productivity and engagement.

Furthermore, leadership and management support can be seen through the encouragement of self-care practices. Encouraging employees to take breaks, use their vacation time, and engage in activities that promote physical and mental well-being are all crucial aspects of fostering a healthy work/life balance. When leaders and managers prioritize their own self-care and openly discuss its benefits, employees are more likely to follow suit, creating a positive ripple effect throughout the organization.

Effective communication is another key component of leadership and management support. Leaders who openly communicate about work/life balance initiatives, policies, and resources available to employees indicate a genuine concern for their well-being. Regular check-ins, performance reviews, and feedback sessions offer opportunities for employees to voice their concerns, seek guidance, and collaboratively find solutions that promote their work/life balance.

Ultimately, leadership and management support are essential elements in creating a workplace culture that values and prioritizes a healthy work/life balance. When employees feel supported and empowered, they are more likely to achieve a sense of harmony between their personal and professional lives. Organizations that actively promote and encourage work/life balance not only attract and retain top talent but also foster an environment where employees thrive, resulting in increased productivity, satisfaction, and overall success.

In today's fast-paced and demanding work environment, achieving a healthy work/life balance is of utmost importance. As employees, we often find ourselves caught in a never-ending cycle of work, with mounting stress and little time for ourselves or our loved ones. This is where leadership and management support play a crucial role in helping us attain a better equilibrium between our professional and personal lives.

The subchapter "Leadership and Management Support" delves into the significance of having strong leaders who prioritize work/life balance and provide the necessary support to employees. This support can be instrumental in fostering a positive work environment and enabling us to lead fulfilling lives both in and outside of the office.

Effective leadership understands that a healthy work/life balance is not only beneficial for individual employees but also for the overall success and productivity of an organization. When leaders actively promote work/life balance, they create a culture that values the well-being of their employees. This, in turn, leads to increased job satisfaction, higher morale, and reduced burnout rates.

Management support plays a crucial role in ensuring that employees have the resources and opportunities to maintain a healthy work/life balance. This can include flexible working arrangements, such as remote work options, compressed workweeks, or flexible scheduling, which allow employees to better manage their personal commitments. By offering these options, employers demonstrate their understanding of the diverse needs and responsibilities of their workforce.

Moreover, leadership and management support also involve fostering an open and transparent communication channel. This allows employees to express their concerns, share their challenges, and seek guidance when needed. When leaders actively listen and provide guidance, employees feel supported and empowered to make informed decisions about their work/life balance.

In conclusion, the subchapter "Leadership and Management Support" emphasizes the crucial role that leaders and managers play in promoting a healthy work/life balance. By prioritizing work/life balance and providing the necessary support, employers create an environment that values employee well-being, leading to increased job satisfaction and productivity. It is essential for employees to advocate for leadership and management support in order to achieve a healthier and more fulfilling work/life balance.

Leading by example in work/life balance

In today's fast-paced and demanding work environment, finding a healthy work/life balance has become more crucial than ever. As employees, we often find ourselves caught up in the never-ending cycle of work, neglecting our personal lives and well-being. However, it is essential to recognize the importance of maintaining a healthy work/life balance and the positive impact it can have on our overall happiness and productivity.

One effective way to encourage and promote work/life balance within an organization is through leading by example. When employers prioritize their own work/life balance, it sends a powerful message to employees that their well-being matters. By demonstrating the importance of finding harmony between work and personal life, employers can inspire their workforce to do the same.

Leading by example in work/life balance involves setting boundaries and creating a culture that supports employees in achieving a healthy balance. This can be done by encouraging employees to take breaks, use vacation time, and avoid working excessive hours. When employers prioritize their own self-care, such as taking regular breaks and vacations, it gives employees permission to do the same without feeling guilty or judged.

Moreover, employers can lead by example by promoting flexible work arrangements. This includes options such as remote work, flexible schedules, and compressed workweeks. By implementing these policies, employers demonstrate their commitment to work/life balance and provide employees with the freedom to manage their time effectively. This flexibility allows employees to fulfill personal obligations, pursue hobbies, and spend quality time with loved ones, resulting in increased job satisfaction and overall well-being.

Additionally, employers can encourage employees to prioritize self-care and personal development. By offering wellness programs, mental health resources, and professional growth opportunities, employers show that they value the holistic well-being of their workforce. This not only enhances employees' work/life balance but also cultivates a positive and supportive work environment.

In conclusion, leading by example in work/life balance is a powerful tool for employers to promote a healthy and balanced lifestyle among employees. By prioritizing their own work/life balance, setting boundaries, and offering flexible work arrangements, employers can inspire their workforce to achieve a healthy equilibrium between work and personal life. This, in turn, leads to increased employee satisfaction, improved productivity, and a positive work environment. Remember, finding a healthy work/life balance is not just a personal responsibility but also an organizational one, and it starts with leading by example.

In today's fast-paced and demanding work environment, achieving a healthy work/life balance has become increasingly important. As employees, we often find ourselves juggling multiple responsibilities both at work and in our personal lives. This subchapter explores the significance of a healthy work/life balance and how leading by example can positively impact our overall well-being.

A healthy work/life balance is crucial for several reasons. First and foremost, it promotes our physical and mental well-being. Balancing our professional and personal lives allows us to recharge, reduce stress levels, and maintain a positive outlook. It enables us to be more present and engaged in all aspects of our lives, leading to increased productivity and job satisfaction.

Moreover, a healthy work/life balance fosters strong relationships with our loved ones. By allocating time for them, we show them that they are a priority in our lives. This, in turn, strengthens our support network and enhances our overall happiness. It also helps us avoid burnout, which can have detrimental effects on our health and relationships.

Leading by example in work/life balance is essential for both employees and employers. When employers demonstrate a commitment to work/life balance, it creates an organizational culture that values the well-being of its employees. This can be achieved through various means, such as offering flexible work arrangements, encouraging breaks and vacations, and promoting open communication.

As employees, we can also play a crucial role in leading by example. By prioritizing our work/life balance, we set a precedent for our colleagues and inspire them to do the same. This can be done by setting boundaries, effectively managing our time, and seeking support when needed. When we demonstrate our ability to achieve a healthy work/life balance, we become role models for others in our organization.

Furthermore, leading by example in work/life balance not only benefits ourselves and our colleagues but also the overall success of our organization. Employees who have a healthy work/life balance are more likely to be motivated, engaged, and committed to their work. They bring fresh perspectives, innovation, and creativity to the table. By prioritizing our well-being, we contribute to a positive work environment that fosters productivity and growth.

In conclusion, a healthy work/life balance is crucial for our overall well-being, relationships, and job satisfaction. Leading by example in work/life balance allows us to create a positive impact on ourselves, our colleagues, and our organization. By prioritizing our well-being and showing others that it is possible to achieve a balance, we contribute to a culture that values work/life balance and promotes the success of all its members.

Training managers to support work/life balance

Training managers to support work/life balance is crucial in today's fast-paced and demanding work environment. As employees, we often find ourselves juggling multiple responsibilities, both at work and in our personal lives. Achieving a healthy work/life balance is essential for our overall well-being and happiness, and it is the responsibility of managers to support us in this pursuit.

First and foremost, it is important for managers to understand the significance of a healthy work/life balance. When employees are overwhelmed with work and do not have time for their personal lives, it can lead to increased stress, burnout, and decreased productivity. By recognizing the importance of work/life balance, managers can create a supportive and inclusive work culture that values the well-being of its employees.

Training managers to support work/life balance involves equipping them with the necessary skills and knowledge. This includes educating them about the benefits of work/life balance, such as increased employee engagement, satisfaction, and retention. Managers should also be trained on how to recognize signs of burnout or excessive stress in employees and how to address these issues effectively.

Additionally, managers should be trained in effective communication and time management techniques. By improving their communication skills, managers can better understand the needs and concerns of their employees and can work together to find solutions that promote work/life balance. Time management training can help managers prioritize tasks, delegate responsibilities, and create realistic timelines, thereby reducing the likelihood of employees feeling overwhelmed.

Furthermore, managers should be trained to lead by example. When employees see their managers actively practicing and promoting work/life balance, it sends a powerful message that it is not only accepted but encouraged within the organization. Managers should be encouraged to take regular breaks, utilize flexible work arrangements, and set boundaries between work and personal life. This will create a positive work environment where employees feel supported in achieving their own work/life balance.

In conclusion, training managers to support work/life balance is essential for creating a healthy and thriving work environment. By recognizing the importance of work/life balance, equipping managers with the necessary skills and knowledge, and leading by example, organizations can foster a culture that values the well-being of its employees. It is through this support that employees can achieve a healthy work/life balance and ultimately lead more fulfilling lives.

In today's fast-paced and demanding work environment, achieving a healthy work/life balance has become essential for employees' overall well-being and productivity. Recognizing the significance of this issue, organizations are increasingly focusing on training their managers to support their employees in maintaining a harmonious work/life balance. This subchapter delves into the importance of training managers in this area and how it can positively impact employees' lives.

A healthy work/life balance is crucial for employees as it contributes to their physical and mental well-being. When individuals have time to relax, pursue personal interests, and spend quality time with their loved ones, they experience reduced stress levels and increased job satisfaction. By training managers to understand and value work/life balance, organizations can create a supportive and inclusive culture that prioritizes employees' happiness and overall success.

One of the key aspects of training managers to support work/life balance is teaching them effective communication skills. Managers need to be able to have open and honest conversations with their team members, discussing workloads, deadlines, and any personal challenges that may impact their ability to find balance. By fostering a culture of open communication, managers can help employees feel comfortable discussing their needs and concerns, ultimately leading to a more supportive work environment.

Training managers to lead by example is another vital component of supporting work/life balance. When managers demonstrate their own commitment to achieving a healthy work/life balance, employees are more likely to feel empowered to do the same. Managers should encourage their teams to take breaks, utilize their vacation time, and establish clear boundaries between work and personal life. By setting a positive example, managers can inspire their employees to prioritize their well-being and achieve a better work/life balance.

Additionally, training managers to implement flexible work arrangements can greatly contribute to supporting work/life balance. By allowing employees to have control over when and where they work, organizations can empower them to better manage their personal obligations and achieve a greater sense of balance. Managers should be trained to assess individual needs and explore flexible options such as remote work, compressed workweeks, or job sharing, whenever feasible.

In conclusion, training managers to support work/life balance is essential in creating a healthy and productive work environment. By equipping managers with effective communication skills, encouraging them to lead by example, and promoting flexible work arrangements, organizations can demonstrate their commitment to the well-being of their employees. Ultimately, by investing in training programs that prioritize work/life balance, organizations can foster a culture that values and supports employees' overall happiness and success.

Communication and Transparency

In today's fast-paced and demanding work environment, maintaining a healthy work/life balance has become more critical than ever. As employees, it can often feel like we are constantly juggling multiple responsibilities, both at work and at home. However, one key aspect that can significantly impact our ability to achieve this balance is effective communication and transparency within the workplace.

Communication and transparency are essential elements in fostering a positive work environment, reducing stress levels, and promoting work/life balance. When employers prioritize open and honest communication, employees feel more connected and engaged. This sense of connection enables them to better manage their workloads and personal commitments, ultimately leading to a healthier work/life balance.

By promoting a culture of open communication, employers allow employees to express their needs and concerns freely. This creates a safe space for discussing work-related issues, personal challenges, or any conflicts that may arise. Regular check-ins, team meetings, and one-on-one conversations are all effective tools that can be utilized to ensure that communication channels are open and accessible to everyone.

Transparency is another vital factor that contributes to a healthy work/life balance. Employers who provide transparent information about company policies, expectations, and decision-making processes empower their employees to make informed choices about how they manage their time and energy. When employees understand the bigger picture, they can better prioritize their tasks and allocate resources accordingly.

Transparent communication also means being honest about limitations and challenges. Employers who acknowledge and address these obstacles help employees feel supported and valued. This recognition allows for more realistic expectations and helps employees avoid burnout or excessive stress.

Moreover, clear communication and transparency reduce uncertainty and ambiguity, which are often sources of anxiety and stress. When employees have a clear understanding of their roles, deadlines, and expectations, they can plan and organize their time more effectively. This clarity enables them to set boundaries and allocate time for personal commitments, leading to a healthier work/life balance.

In conclusion, effective communication and transparency are essential components in achieving a healthy work/life balance. Employers who prioritize open and honest communication create a supportive work environment where employees feel heard and valued. By promoting transparency, employers enable employees to make informed choices, manage their time efficiently, and maintain a healthy equilibrium between work and personal life. Embracing these principles will not only benefit the employees but also contribute to a more productive and harmonious workplace.

Open dialogue on work/life balance

In today's fast-paced and demanding world, achieving a healthy work/life balance has become increasingly important. As employees, we often find ourselves caught up in the never-ending cycle of work commitments, deadlines, and personal responsibilities. It is crucial to open up a dialogue about work/life balance and understand its significance in order to lead fulfilling and productive lives.

A healthy work/life balance refers to the equilibrium between our professional and personal lives. It is about finding the right blend that allows us to excel in our careers while also nurturing our personal well-being, relationships, and overall happiness. However, striking this balance can be challenging, especially when work demands seem to outweigh other aspects of our lives.

By engaging in an open dialogue about work/life balance, we can create awareness and foster a supportive environment within our workplaces. This dialogue should encourage employees to share their experiences, challenges, and ideas, allowing for a collective understanding of the importance of achieving balance.

One of the primary benefits of a healthy work/life balance is improved mental and physical well-being. When we prioritize self-care and give ourselves time to relax and rejuvenate, we become more resilient and better equipped to handle the demands of our professional lives. This, in turn, leads to increased productivity, creativity, and job satisfaction.

Moreover, a balanced approach to work and life helps us build and nurture meaningful relationships. It allows us to spend quality time with our loved ones, engage in hobbies, and pursue personal interests.

By fostering these connections and activities, we enhance our overall happiness and satisfaction, leading to a more fulfilled and successful life.

Additionally, open dialogue about work/life balance creates an opportunity for employers to understand the unique needs and challenges faced by their employees. This understanding can lead to the implementation of flexible work arrangements, such as remote work options, flexible hours, or compressed workweeks. These initiatives promote work/life balance and can significantly improve employee well-being, engagement, and retention.

In conclusion, an open dialogue on work/life balance is crucial for employees to recognize the importance of achieving a healthy equilibrium between their professional and personal lives. By engaging in discussions about this topic, we can raise awareness, share experiences, and foster a supportive environment within our workplaces. A healthy work/life balance ultimately leads to improved mental and physical well-being, enhanced relationships, and increased overall happiness and job satisfaction. It is essential for employers to be receptive to these conversations and implement flexible work arrangements that promote work/life balance, benefiting both employees and the organization as a whole.

Sharing resources and information

In today's fast-paced and interconnected world, the sharing of resources and information has become more crucial than ever. As employees, we often find ourselves overwhelmed with the demands of work and struggle to maintain a healthy work-life balance. However, by embracing the concept of sharing resources and information, we can effectively navigate the challenges and find harmony between our professional and personal lives.

One of the key benefits of sharing resources is the ability to lighten the load. In our workplaces, there is often a wealth of knowledge and expertise that can be tapped into. By creating a culture of sharing, we can leverage the collective wisdom of our colleagues and find innovative solutions to problems. Instead of reinventing the wheel, we can learn from others' experiences and save valuable time and effort. Whether it is through formal training programs, mentorship opportunities, or simply sharing best practices, the sharing of resources empowers us to work smarter, not harder.

Furthermore, sharing information fosters collaboration and teamwork. When we openly communicate with our colleagues, we create an environment of trust and transparency. This enables us to work together more effectively, pooling our strengths and supporting one another. By sharing information about projects, deadlines, and priorities, we can align our efforts, avoid duplication, and achieve better outcomes. Additionally, sharing information about personal commitments and responsibilities outside of work can help our colleagues better understand our needs and offer support when needed, further enhancing our work-life balance.

In the digital age, technology has made sharing resources and information easier than ever before. With the advent of collaborative platforms and communication tools, we can connect with our colleagues regardless of geographical boundaries. We can access shared documents, participate in virtual meetings, and engage in real-time discussions, all of which enable seamless collaboration and knowledge sharing. By harnessing these tools, we can truly embrace the power of flexibility, as we can work from anywhere, at any time, while still maintaining a healthy work-life balance.

In conclusion, sharing resources and information is vital for maintaining a healthy work-life balance. By tapping into the collective wisdom of our colleagues, we can find innovative solutions, work more efficiently, and achieve better outcomes. Through open communication and collaboration, we can build strong relationships and support one another. Embracing technology allows us to connect and share seamlessly, regardless of physical location. So let us seize the power of sharing and create a culture of collaboration in our workplaces, enabling us to shape our work-life balance and thrive both personally and professionally.

Chapter 6: Overcoming Challenges and Obstacles

Addressing Workload and Burnout

Achieving a healthy work/life balance is crucial for overall well-being and success. In today's fast-paced and demanding work environment, it's common for employees to feel overwhelmed and burnt out due to excessive workload. However, by understanding the importance of addressing workload and burnout, we can take proactive steps to create a healthier work environment and maintain a better work/life balance.

First and foremost, it's important to recognize the signs of burnout. Feeling constantly exhausted, experiencing increased cynicism or detachment from work, and a decline in productivity are all indicators that you may be facing burnout. By identifying these signs early on, you can take necessary action to address the root causes and prevent it from escalating further.

One effective approach to addressing workload and burnout is open communication. Employees should feel comfortable discussing their workload concerns with their supervisors or managers. By having an open dialogue, you can work together to find solutions that alleviate excessive workload and create a more manageable work environment. This may involve redistributing tasks, setting realistic deadlines, or exploring opportunities for skill development and delegation.

Another key aspect is time management. Learning how to prioritize tasks and set boundaries can significantly impact your work/life balance. By effectively managing your time, you can ensure that you allocate adequate time for both work and personal life, reducing the risk of burnout. Techniques like breaking tasks into smaller, manageable chunks and setting clear goals can help you stay organized and focused, ultimately improving productivity and reducing stress levels.

Employers also play a crucial role in addressing workload and burnout. They should actively promote work/life balance by implementing policies and practices that support their employees' well-being. This includes providing opportunities for flexible work arrangements, encouraging breaks throughout the workday, and promoting a positive and supportive work culture.

Additionally, employers can offer resources and support systems to help employees manage their workload and prevent burnout. This may include training on stress management techniques, providing access to employee assistance programs, or organizing wellness initiatives such as yoga or meditation sessions.

In conclusion, addressing workload and burnout is essential for maintaining a healthy work/life balance. By recognizing the signs of burnout, fostering open communication, practicing effective time management, and promoting supportive work environments, both employees and employers can work together to create a better work experience that prioritizes well-being and productivity. Remember, a healthy work/life balance is not just a luxury but a necessity for long-term success and personal happiness.

Strategies for managing heavy workloads

In today's fast-paced and demanding work environment, managing heavy workloads can often be a challenging task. As employees, it is crucial to find effective strategies that help us maintain a healthy work/life balance. This subchapter aims to provide you with practical strategies to tackle heavy workloads while ensuring that you prioritize your well-being and personal life.

1. Prioritize and Plan: Start by assessing your workload and breaking it down into smaller, manageable tasks. Prioritize your tasks based on urgency and importance. Create a to-do list or use project management tools to keep track of your progress. Planning ahead will help you stay organized and focused on the most critical tasks.

2. Delegate and Collaborate: Recognize when you can't handle everything on your own. Delegate tasks to capable colleagues or team members. Collaboration not only lightens your load but also promotes teamwork and fosters a supportive work environment. Effective communication and clear expectations are key when delegating or collaborating on tasks.

3. Time Management: Efficiently managing your time is vital in handling heavy workloads. Identify your peak productivity hours and schedule your most demanding tasks during these times. Avoid multitasking as it can lead to decreased productivity and increased stress. Instead, practice time blocking by dedicating specific time slots to different tasks, allowing you to focus on one task at a time.

4. Set Boundaries: Establish clear boundaries between work and personal life. Avoid overworking by setting realistic expectations with

your employer and colleagues. Learn to say no to additional tasks when you are already overloaded. Remember, it is essential to take breaks and recharge to maintain productivity and overall well-being.

5. Seek Support: Reach out to your supervisor, mentor, or HR department when you are struggling with heavy workloads. They can provide guidance, offer additional resources, or even reevaluate your workload if necessary. Don't hesitate to ask for help or express your concerns. Seeking support demonstrates your commitment to maintaining a healthy work/life balance.

6. Self-Care: Prioritize self-care activities that promote relaxation and reduce stress. Engage in regular exercise, practice mindfulness or meditation, and ensure you get enough sleep. Taking care of your physical and mental well-being is crucial in managing heavy workloads effectively.

In conclusion, managing heavy workloads requires a combination of effective strategies and a commitment to maintaining a healthy work/life balance. By prioritizing tasks, delegating when necessary, managing your time, setting boundaries, seeking support, and practicing self-care, you can navigate through heavy workloads while preserving your well-being and personal life. Remember, a balanced approach to work and life contributes to long-term success and overall happiness.

Identifying signs of burnout and seeking support

In today's fast-paced and demanding work environment, achieving a healthy work/life balance is more crucial than ever. As employees, it is essential to recognize the signs of burnout and seek the necessary support to maintain our overall well-being. This subchapter explores the importance of identifying these signs and provides guidance on seeking the support we need.

Burnout is a state of chronic physical and emotional exhaustion caused by prolonged exposure to high levels of stress. It can affect anyone, regardless of their role or industry. However, it is often associated with individuals who constantly push themselves to their limits without taking time to recharge. Recognizing the signs of burnout is the first step towards preventing it from taking a toll on our lives.

Some common signs of burnout include fatigue, decreased productivity, and a feeling of cynicism towards work. You may also experience physical symptoms such as headaches, insomnia, or changes in appetite. Additionally, burnout can lead to emotional exhaustion, feelings of detachment, and a loss of interest in activities you once enjoyed. It is crucial to pay attention to these signs and take them seriously.

Seeking support is vital when dealing with burnout. Remember, you are not alone in this journey. Start by reaching out to your manager or supervisor to discuss your concerns openly. They may be able to offer solutions such as adjusting your workload, providing additional resources, or suggesting time off to recharge.

If you find it challenging to speak with your manager directly, consider seeking support from your colleagues, friends, or family members. Sometimes, just talking about your feelings and experiences can provide relief and help you gain a fresh perspective. Additionally, consider utilizing employee assistance programs or counseling services that your company may offer. These resources can provide professional guidance and support tailored to your specific needs.

Preventing burnout is not only beneficial for your well-being but also for your overall performance and satisfaction in your role. By actively identifying the signs of burnout and seeking support, you can maintain a healthy work/life balance and thrive both personally and professionally.

Remember, it is essential to prioritize self-care and set boundaries to prevent burnout. Take breaks, engage in activities that bring you joy, and ensure you have a support system in place. By doing so, you are investing in your well-being and empowering yourself to excel in both your personal and professional life.

Overcoming Stigma and Cultural Barriers

In today's fast-paced and demanding work environment, finding the right balance between work and personal life has become increasingly crucial for individuals' overall well-being. However, achieving this equilibrium can be challenging due to various factors, including stigma and cultural barriers. In this subchapter, we will delve into the importance of overcoming these obstacles and provide practical strategies for employees to create a healthy work/life balance.

Stigma surrounding work/life balance is a pervasive issue that can hinder individuals from prioritizing their personal lives. Many employees fear that seeking a better balance may be perceived as a lack of commitment or dedication to their work. This misconception often leads to long working hours, burnout, and a decline in overall productivity. To break free from this stigma, it is crucial for employees to recognize that a healthy work/life balance is not synonymous with laziness or lack of ambition. Instead, it is a vital component for maintaining physical and mental well-being, enhancing productivity, and fostering personal growth.

Cultural barriers can also significantly impact an individual's ability to achieve a healthy work/life balance. Different cultures have varying perspectives on the importance of work and the role it plays in one's life. Some cultures may prioritize work above all else, leaving little room for personal time and leisure activities. Recognizing and addressing these cultural barriers is essential for employees seeking a better work/life balance.

One effective strategy for overcoming stigma and cultural barriers is open communication. Employees should feel empowered to discuss their work/life balance needs with their supervisors, colleagues, and even family members. By openly expressing their desires for a healthier balance, individuals can help educate others about the benefits and dispel any misconceptions or stigmas associated with it.

Another strategy is to set clear boundaries between work and personal life. Establishing specific working hours and avoiding work-related activities during personal time can help create a clearer separation between the two. Additionally, employees should make a conscious effort to prioritize self-care and leisure activities, ensuring they allocate sufficient time for relaxation, hobbies, and spending quality time with loved ones.

In conclusion, overcoming stigma and cultural barriers is crucial for employees striving to achieve a healthy work/life balance. By challenging misconceptions and openly communicating their needs, individuals can create a supportive environment that values personal well-being alongside professional success. Setting clear boundaries and prioritizing self-care are also essential steps towards maintaining a sustainable work/life balance. Remember, a healthy work/life balance is not a sign of weakness or lack of commitment; it is a fundamental aspect of living a fulfilling and productive life.

Challenging societal norms and expectations

In today's fast-paced and demanding world, striking a healthy work/life balance has become increasingly important. Many of us find ourselves caught in a web of societal norms and expectations that dictate how we should live our lives and prioritize our time. However, it is crucial for employees to challenge these norms and take control of their own work/life balance in order to lead fulfilling and satisfying lives.

Societal norms often dictate that success is measured solely by professional achievements and material possessions. This can lead to a constant pressure to work longer hours, take on more responsibilities, and sacrifice personal well-being for the sake of career advancement. However, research has shown that a healthy work/life balance is essential for overall happiness and well-being.

By challenging societal norms and expectations, employees can prioritize their personal lives and mental health without compromising their professional success. Instead of striving for an unrealistic work-life balance, individuals should strive for a healthy integration of both aspects of their lives. This means setting boundaries, learning to say no, and prioritizing self-care.

Employers play a crucial role in shaping work/life balance by creating a supportive and flexible work environment. Forward-thinking companies understand that employees who have a healthy work/life balance are more productive, engaged, and satisfied in their roles. They provide benefits such as flexible working hours, remote work options, and wellness programs to help employees achieve this balance.

It is essential for employees to communicate their needs and expectations to their employers. By advocating for a healthy work/life balance, employees can challenge societal norms and help create a more inclusive and supportive work culture. This may involve having open conversations about the importance of personal time, mental health, and the need for flexibility.

Ultimately, challenging societal norms and expectations is a powerful step towards achieving a healthy work/life balance. By prioritizing personal well-being alongside professional success, employees can lead more fulfilling lives and contribute to a positive work culture. It is time to break free from the chains of societal expectations and embrace a more flexible and balanced approach to work and life.

Fostering inclusivity and diversity in work/life balance initiatives

In today's fast-paced and demanding work environment, achieving a healthy work/life balance has become increasingly crucial for employees. Recognizing the importance of a healthy work/life balance, employers are now implementing various initiatives to support their workforce. However, it is equally essential for these initiatives to promote inclusivity and diversity, ensuring that every employee's unique needs and circumstances are acknowledged and addressed.

An inclusive work/life balance initiative goes beyond offering flexible working hours or remote work options. It aims to create an environment where all employees feel valued and supported, regardless of their gender, race, age, disability, or background. By fostering inclusivity and diversity, employers can enhance the overall effectiveness and success of their work/life balance initiatives.

One way to foster inclusivity and diversity is by conducting regular surveys or feedback sessions to understand the needs and challenges faced by different employee groups. This will help employers identify any gaps or areas for improvement in their current initiatives. By actively seeking input from employees, companies can ensure that their work/life balance policies are tailored to meet the diverse needs of their workforce.

Another important aspect is providing equal opportunities for career advancement and professional development. Inclusivity means creating a level playing field where every employee has the chance to succeed and grow. Employers can support this by offering mentorship programs, training opportunities, and networking events that are accessible and inclusive to all employees. By investing in the development of a diverse workforce, companies can foster an inclusive culture that promotes work/life balance for everyone.

Additionally, employers should strive to eliminate any biases or stereotypes that may hinder inclusivity and diversity in work/life balance initiatives. This can be achieved through diversity and inclusion training programs that promote empathy, understanding, and respect among employees. By addressing unconscious biases and promoting a culture of acceptance, employers can create an environment where everyone feels comfortable and supported in their work/life balance choices.

Ultimately, fostering inclusivity and diversity in work/life balance initiatives is not just a moral imperative, but also a strategic move for employers. By embracing the unique needs of their diverse workforce, companies can attract and retain top talent, drive innovation, and enhance employee satisfaction and productivity. It is through such initiatives that employers truly harness the power of flexibility and shape a truly inclusive work environment.

Chapter 7: Sustainable Work/Life Balance

Maintaining Work/Life Balance in the Long Term

In today's fast-paced and demanding world, finding a healthy work/life balance has become more crucial than ever. As employees, we often find ourselves juggling multiple responsibilities and commitments, both personally and professionally. However, neglecting our personal lives for the sake of work can have detrimental effects on our overall well-being. This subchapter aims to shed light on the importance of maintaining a healthy work/life balance in the long term, providing practical tips and strategies to achieve equilibrium.

1. Prioritizing self-care: It is essential to prioritize self-care to maintain a healthy work/life balance. Engaging in activities that rejuvenate and recharge us, such as exercising, pursuing hobbies, and spending quality time with loved ones, can help us create a sense of fulfillment and happiness outside of work.

2. Setting boundaries: Establishing clear boundaries between work and personal life is crucial. This involves setting realistic expectations with employers, colleagues, and even ourselves. Learning to say no when necessary and not overcommitting can help prevent burnout and ensure adequate time for personal pursuits.

3. Effective time management: Efficiently managing our time is instrumental in maintaining work/life balance. By prioritizing tasks and setting realistic goals, we can avoid feeling overwhelmed and stay organized. Utilizing time management techniques, such as the

Pomodoro Technique or creating to-do lists, can enhance productivity and enable us to allocate time for personal activities.

4. Establishing a support network: Building a strong support network can significantly contribute to maintaining work/life balance. Surrounding ourselves with understanding friends, family, and colleagues who value the importance of work/life balance can provide the necessary encouragement and assistance when needed.

5. Embracing flexibility: Embracing flexibility in our work arrangements can be instrumental in achieving work/life balance. Discussing flexible working options, such as remote work or flexible hours, with employers can help accommodate personal commitments and create a healthier work environment.

6. Mindfulness and stress management: Practicing mindfulness techniques, such as meditation or deep breathing exercises, can help reduce stress and promote a sense of calmness. Incorporating stress management techniques into our daily routines can enhance our ability to navigate work and personal challenges effectively.

7. Regular reflection and reassessment: Regularly reflecting on our work/life balance and reassessing our priorities is essential to ensure long-term equilibrium. As circumstances change, it is important to evaluate our goals and make necessary adjustments to align with our desired work/life balance.

By actively prioritizing and maintaining a healthy work/life balance, employees can experience increased satisfaction, improved mental and physical well-being, and enhanced productivity in both their personal and professional lives. The key lies in taking proactive steps, setting boundaries, and embracing flexibility to create a harmonious and fulfilling life.

Strategies for sustaining work/life balance

In today's fast-paced and demanding world, achieving a healthy work/life balance has become increasingly challenging. Many employees find themselves caught in a never-ending cycle of work-related stress and obligations, neglecting their personal lives and overall well-being. However, it is crucial to prioritize and sustain a healthy work/life balance to lead a fulfilling and rewarding life. This subchapter will explore effective strategies that employees can adopt to achieve and maintain this balance.

1. Prioritize Self-Care: Remember that self-care is not selfish, but rather a necessary component of maintaining overall well-being. Make time for activities that recharge and rejuvenate you, such as exercise, hobbies, spending time with loved ones, or engaging in mindfulness practices. By prioritizing self-care, you will be better equipped to handle work-related challenges and find a sense of balance.

2. Set Boundaries: Establish clear boundaries between work and personal life. Avoid bringing work-related stress or tasks into your personal time. Define specific working hours and strive to stick to them. Communicate these boundaries to your colleagues and supervisors, ensuring that they respect your personal time as well.

3. Learn to Delegate and Say No: Many employees struggle with taking on too much responsibility due to fear of disappointing others or sacrificing career progress. However, it is crucial to learn how to delegate tasks effectively and to say no when additional commitments would jeopardize your work/life balance. Prioritize your workload and focus on tasks that align with your goals and values.

4. Utilize Flexibility Options: Explore flexible work arrangements offered by your employer, such as remote work, flexible hours, or compressed workweeks. These options can help you better manage your time and integrate work with personal responsibilities, ultimately contributing to a healthier work/life balance.

5. Communicate Openly: Maintain open and honest communication with your employer, colleagues, and loved ones about your work/life balance needs and challenges. By expressing your concerns and seeking support, you can foster a supportive work environment and gain valuable insights and perspectives.

6. Practice Stress Management Techniques: Incorporate stress management techniques into your daily routine, such as deep breathing exercises, meditation, or journaling. These practices can help you remain calm and centered, even during high-pressure work situations.

Remember, achieving and sustaining a healthy work/life balance is an ongoing process that requires conscious effort and self-reflection. By implementing these strategies, you can proactively shape your work/life balance and create a more fulfilling and rewarding life for yourself.

Adjusting to changing personal and professional circumstances

In today's fast-paced and ever-changing world, it is crucial for employees to adapt and adjust to the shifts in their personal and professional lives. The ability to navigate through these changing circumstances is essential for maintaining a healthy work/life balance. In this subchapter, we will explore the importance of adjusting to these changes and provide practical tips for successfully managing them.

First and foremost, it is important to acknowledge that personal and professional circumstances are constantly evolving. From starting a family to pursuing higher education or dealing with unexpected life events, these changes can significantly impact our daily lives. Failing to adapt to these changes can lead to burnout, stress, and a compromised work/life balance. Therefore, it is crucial for employees to develop the skills necessary to adjust and thrive in the face of change.

One key aspect of adjusting to changing circumstances is maintaining open communication with your employer. By keeping them informed about significant life events or personal challenges, you can work together to find solutions that benefit both parties. Employers are increasingly recognizing the importance of a healthy work/life balance and are often willing to offer flexible options or adjust work arrangements to accommodate changing needs.

Additionally, it is essential to prioritize self-care during times of change. This includes taking care of your physical and mental well-being. Engaging in regular exercise, practicing mindfulness, and seeking support from friends, family, or professionals can greatly enhance your ability to adapt to changing circumstances. Remember that taking care of yourself is not a selfish act but one that allows you to show up as your best self in both your personal and professional life.

Flexibility and adaptability are becoming highly valued skills in the workplace. Employers are increasingly recognizing that employees who can successfully adjust to changing circumstances are more productive, engaged, and satisfied. By embracing change and actively seeking opportunities for growth, you demonstrate your willingness to evolve and contribute to the success of your organization.

In summary, adjusting to changing personal and professional circumstances is crucial for maintaining a healthy work/life balance. By communicating openly with your employer, prioritizing self-care, and embracing flexibility, you can navigate through these changes successfully. Remember that change is inevitable, but with the right mindset and strategies, you can adapt and thrive in both your personal and professional life.

Measuring the Impact of Work/Life Balance Initiatives

In today's fast-paced and demanding work environment, achieving a healthy work/life balance has become increasingly crucial for employees. Employers are recognizing the significance of providing initiatives that promote this balance, as it not only benefits the well-being of their workforce but also enhances productivity and job satisfaction. In this subchapter, we will explore the importance of work/life balance and how employers can measure the impact of their initiatives.

A healthy work/life balance refers to the equilibrium between one's professional and personal life. It is about allocating time and energy to both work-related responsibilities and personal commitments, such as family, hobbies, and self-care. Achieving this balance is instrumental in reducing stress, preventing burnout, and fostering overall well-being.

Employers have a vested interest in promoting work/life balance among their employees. Research consistently demonstrates that employees with a healthy balance are more engaged, motivated, and productive. They are also less likely to experience absenteeism or turnover, resulting in cost savings for organizations. Moreover, a positive work/life balance enhances job satisfaction, leading to higher retention rates and improved employee morale.

To measure the impact of work/life balance initiatives, employers can utilize various tools and strategies. One effective method is conducting employee surveys or feedback sessions to gauge their satisfaction and perceptions of the initiatives. By collecting quantitative and qualitative data, organizations can assess the effectiveness of their programs and identify areas for improvement.

Another valuable measurement tool is tracking key performance indicators (KPIs) related to productivity, absenteeism, and turnover. Comparing these metrics before and after implementing work/life balance initiatives can provide insights into the impact they have on employee performance and retention.

Additionally, organizations can analyze data from employee assistance programs, wellness initiatives, and flexible work arrangements to evaluate their effectiveness. By examining the utilization rates, employee feedback, and overall program outcomes, employers can determine if their initiatives are positively influencing work/life balance.

In conclusion, maintaining a healthy work/life balance is vital for employees' overall well-being and organizational success. Employers play a crucial role in shaping work environments that promote this balance through various initiatives. Measuring the impact of these initiatives allows organizations to assess their effectiveness, make informed decisions, and continually improve the work/life balance offerings. By prioritizing work/life balance, both employees and employers can reap the benefits of enhanced productivity, job satisfaction, and overall happiness.

Collecting feedback and evaluating effectiveness

Collecting Feedback and Evaluating Effectiveness: Enhancing Work/Life Balance

In today's fast-paced and demanding work environment, maintaining a healthy work/life balance has become increasingly vital. As employees, it is essential to recognize the significance of this equilibrium and the positive impact it can have on our overall well-being. To achieve this balance, it is crucial to collect feedback and evaluate its effectiveness regularly. This subchapter delves into the importance of gathering feedback and understanding its role in shaping a healthy work/life balance.

Feedback is a powerful tool that allows employees to voice their opinions, concerns, and suggestions regarding their work/life balance. By actively seeking feedback from employees, organizations can gain valuable insights into the effectiveness of their work/life balance initiatives. Employers need to create a safe and supportive environment where employees feel comfortable sharing their thoughts without fear of negative consequences. This will enable organizations to make informed decisions and implement necessary changes to enhance work/life balance.

One of the most effective ways to collect feedback is through surveys or questionnaires. These tools provide employees with a structured platform to express their experiences, challenges, and suggestions. Questions can focus on various aspects such as workload distribution, flexible work arrangements, support systems, and the impact of work on personal life. By analyzing the responses, employers can identify patterns, trends, and areas that need improvement.

Additionally, employers should establish open lines of communication to encourage ongoing feedback. Regular check-ins, one-on-one meetings, and team discussions provide opportunities for employees to express their thoughts and concerns. This continuous dialogue ensures that employees feel heard, fostering a culture of mutual understanding and support.

It is equally important for organizations to evaluate the effectiveness of their work/life balance initiatives. Regular assessments help determine if the implemented strategies are meeting the desired outcomes and identify areas for improvement. This evaluation process may involve analyzing key performance indicators, reviewing feedback trends, and conducting focus groups or interviews. Employers can then make data-driven decisions to refine existing policies or introduce new initiatives that better support work/life balance.

In conclusion, collecting feedback and evaluating its effectiveness play a pivotal role in shaping a healthy work/life balance. Employees should actively participate in providing feedback, enabling organizations to make informed decisions that enhance their overall well-being. By creating an environment that encourages open communication and regularly assessing work/life balance initiatives, employers can ensure that their employees' needs are met, resulting in increased job satisfaction, productivity, and overall happiness.

Making improvements based on employee input

In today's fast-paced and demanding work environment, it is crucial for employers to understand the importance of a healthy work/life balance. Employees around the world are constantly seeking ways to strike a balance between their personal and professional lives. As an employee, it is essential to communicate your needs and concerns to your employer to ensure a harmonious work/life balance. This subchapter will explore the significance of making improvements based on employee input and how it can positively impact your overall well-being.

Your employer's willingness to listen and consider your input is a clear sign of their commitment to your well-being. When employers actively seek feedback from their employees, they create an environment that promotes trust, transparency, and collaboration. By valuing your input, employers can identify areas where changes can be made to improve work/life balance, resulting in increased job satisfaction and productivity.

One of the main benefits of making improvements based on employee input is that it allows for a more tailored and personalized approach to work/life balance. No two individuals have the same needs or responsibilities outside of work. By taking your input into account, your employer can implement policies and practices that accommodate your specific circumstances. This may include flexible working hours, remote work options, or additional support for personal commitments, such as childcare or eldercare.

Furthermore, when employers actively seek employee input, it fosters a culture of continuous improvement. Your insights and suggestions can lead to innovative solutions that benefit not only you but the entire organization. Employers who value employee feedback are more likely to adapt and evolve their policies to meet the changing needs of their workforce. This, in turn, creates a positive work environment that attracts and retains top talent.

To ensure that your input is heard, it is important to actively participate in any feedback mechanisms established by your employer. This may include surveys, suggestion boxes, or regular meetings with management. Be honest and open about your needs, concerns, and ideas for improvement. Remember, your employer wants to create an environment that supports your work/life balance, but they can only do so if they are aware of your specific needs.

In conclusion, making improvements based on employee input is vital for achieving a healthy work/life balance. By actively seeking your input, employers can create a workplace that values your well-being and supports your personal commitments. Remember to communicate your needs and ideas to your employer, as your input can lead to positive changes that benefit both you and the organization as a whole.

Chapter 8: The Future of Work/Life Balance

Trends and Innovations in Work/Life Balance

In today's fast-paced and demanding work environment, achieving a healthy work/life balance has become more important than ever. As employees, we often find ourselves juggling multiple responsibilities, both at work and in our personal lives. This subchapter explores the latest trends and innovations in work/life balance, shedding light on how employers are shaping this crucial aspect of our lives.

One of the key trends in work/life balance is the rise of flexible work arrangements. Gone are the days when employees were confined to a traditional 9-to-5 schedule. Employers have recognized the need for more flexibility, allowing employees to customize their work hours and location. This shift has been made possible by the advancements in technology, which enable employees to work remotely and collaborate seamlessly with their colleagues. Whether it's working from home, having flexible start and end times, or even compressed workweeks, these arrangements provide employees with the freedom to manage their personal obligations while still meeting their professional responsibilities.

Another innovative approach to work/life balance is the implementation of wellness programs in the workplace. Employers have recognized that a healthy employee is a productive employee, and as such, they are investing in programs that promote physical, mental, and emotional well-being. This can range from on-site fitness facilities, yoga classes, and meditation rooms to mental health support programs and stress management workshops. By creating an environment that supports employee wellness, employers are not only fostering a healthier workforce but also sending a clear message that they value the overall well-being of their employees.

Additionally, employers are increasingly offering benefits that support work/life balance. These can include generous parental leave policies, flexible vacation and paid time off, and even sabbatical programs. By providing these benefits, employers acknowledge the importance of taking time away from work to recharge and spend quality time with loved ones. Moreover, some companies are now offering additional perks such as childcare assistance, elder care support, and even pet-friendly policies, recognizing the diverse needs and responsibilities of their employees.

In conclusion, the trends and innovations in work/life balance are transforming the way we approach our professional and personal lives. Employers are taking proactive steps to create a supportive environment that acknowledges and values the importance of a healthy work/life balance. As employees, it is crucial for us to stay informed about these trends and take advantage of the opportunities provided by our employers. By striking a balance between work and personal life, we can lead happier, healthier, and more fulfilling lives.

Remote work advancements and technology

Remote work advancements and technology have revolutionized the way we work and have become increasingly important in achieving a healthy work/life balance. In today's fast-paced world, where technology is rapidly evolving, employees are no longer confined to traditional office settings. Instead, they have the flexibility to work remotely, whether it be from home, a coworking space, or even while traveling. This subchapter explores the various advancements in remote work and the technology that enables it.

One of the key technological advancements that have paved the way for remote work is the internet. With a stable internet connection, employees can communicate with colleagues and clients, access company files and documents, and collaborate on projects from anywhere in the world. This has not only increased productivity but has also provided employees with the freedom to choose their work environment, allowing them to strike a healthy work/life balance.

Alongside the internet, numerous communication tools have emerged to facilitate seamless remote collaboration. Instant messaging platforms, video conferencing tools, and project management software have become essential for remote teams to stay connected and coordinate their efforts effectively. These tools bridge the gap between physical distance and enable employees to work together as if they were in the same office, fostering a sense of belonging and camaraderie.

Furthermore, cloud computing has revolutionized the storage and sharing of data. With cloud-based platforms, employees can access files and documents securely from any device, eliminating the need for physical storage and making remote work more efficient. This advancement also ensures that employees have access to the most up-to-date information, even when they are not physically present in the office.

Advancements in technology have also given rise to virtual reality (VR) and augmented reality (AR), which have the potential to further enhance remote work experiences. VR and AR can create immersive work environments, enabling employees to feel as if they are in the same physical space, regardless of their actual locations. This can enhance collaboration, creativity, and problem-solving, ultimately contributing to a healthier work/life balance.

In conclusion, remote work advancements and technology have revolutionized the way we work, offering employees the flexibility to choose their work environment and striking a healthy work/life balance. The internet, communication tools, cloud computing, and emerging technologies like VR and AR have made remote work seamless and efficient. As employees, it is essential to embrace these advancements and leverage them to achieve a better work/life balance.

Evolving policies and practices

Evolving Policies and Practices: Creating a Healthy Work/Life Balance

In today's fast-paced and demanding world, finding the right balance between work and personal life has become increasingly important. Employers are recognizing the significance of supporting their employees' well-being, leading to the evolution of policies and practices that promote a healthy work/life balance. This subchapter aims to explore the changing landscape of workplace flexibility and its positive impact on employees.

The Importance of a Healthy Work/Life Balance

A healthy work/life balance is crucial for overall well-being and happiness. It allows individuals to maintain their physical, mental, and emotional health while pursuing their professional goals. Striking this balance is essential to prevent burnout, increase productivity, and foster healthy relationships – both at home and in the workplace.

Recognizing the significance of a work/life balance, employers have started implementing policies and practices that support their employees' well-being. These initiatives acknowledge that employees are not just cogs in a machine, but individuals with personal lives, passions, and responsibilities beyond the workplace.

Evolving Policies and Practices

Over the years, organizations have realized that rigidity in work schedules and expectations can hinder employees' ability to achieve a healthy work/life balance. Consequently, they have adopted more flexible policies and practices to accommodate the diverse needs and lifestyles of their workforce.

Telecommuting and remote work options have gained popularity, allowing employees to work from home or other locations, reducing commuting time and increasing flexibility. This not only saves employees' time and energy but also contributes to a more sustainable environment.

Flexible work hours are another aspect of evolving policies. Employers are recognizing the importance of allowing employees to adjust their schedules to meet personal obligations, such as childcare or attending medical appointments. The ability to adapt work hours to individual needs fosters a sense of autonomy and control over one's life.

Moreover, some organizations have introduced job sharing, part-time work, and compressed workweeks. These options provide employees with opportunities to achieve work/life balance by reducing their working hours without sacrificing career growth or financial stability.

In addition to these policies, companies are increasingly offering wellness programs that focus on physical and mental health. These programs include gym memberships, mental health resources, counseling services, and mindfulness programs. By prioritizing employee well-being, organizations are not only investing in their workforce but also creating a positive and supportive work culture.

Conclusion

The evolution of policies and practices surrounding work/life balance reflects a growing awareness of the importance of employee well-being. Employers are realizing that a healthy work/life balance is not only beneficial for individuals but also for the overall success of the organization. By embracing flexibility and implementing supportive initiatives, employers can create an environment that promotes employee happiness, productivity, and long-term success.

Advocating for Work/Life Balance Rights

In today's fast-paced and demanding work environment, the concept of work/life balance has become increasingly important. As employees, it is crucial to understand the significance of maintaining a healthy work/life balance and advocating for our rights in achieving this equilibrium. This subchapter aims to shed light on the importance of work/life balance and provide guidance on how to advocate for these rights effectively.

A healthy work/life balance is essential for our overall well-being and productivity. It enables us to juggle our personal and professional responsibilities effectively, leading to lower stress levels, improved mental health, and increased job satisfaction. When we prioritize our personal lives alongside work, we can foster stronger relationships with our loved ones, pursue hobbies and interests, and take care of our physical and mental health. This balance enhances our ability to perform at our best and achieve our goals, both personally and professionally.

Advocating for work/life balance rights starts with recognizing that we have the right to a fulfilling personal life outside of work. It is crucial to communicate our needs and boundaries to our employers, making them aware of the importance of work/life balance and how it positively impacts our productivity and well-being. Engaging in open and honest conversations with our supervisors and human resources department can help create a supportive work environment that values work/life balance.

Additionally, employees can join forces by forming or joining employee resource groups that advocate for work/life balance rights. These groups can raise awareness, propose policy changes, and collaborate with management to implement flexible work arrangements, such as remote work options, flexible hours, or compressed workweeks. By actively participating in these initiatives, we can collectively promote a culture that values work/life balance and supports employees in achieving it.

Furthermore, staying informed about labor laws and regulations related to work/life balance is crucial. Understanding our rights and legal protections allows us to confidently address any potential violations or discrepancies in our workplace. By being proactive and well-informed, we can advocate for our rights effectively and foster a healthier work environment for all.

In conclusion, advocating for work/life balance rights is vital for employees seeking to achieve a healthy equilibrium between their personal and professional lives. By recognizing the importance of work/life balance, engaging in open communication with employers, joining employee resource groups, and staying informed about labor laws, we can create a workplace that values and supports work/life balance. Ultimately, prioritizing our well-being and advocating for our rights leads to increased job satisfaction, improved mental health, and a more fulfilling personal life.

Employee rights and legal protections

Employee rights and legal protections are essential aspects of maintaining a healthy work/life balance. In today's fast-paced and demanding work environment, it is crucial for employees to be aware of their rights and the legal protections available to them. This subchapter delves into the significance of employee rights and the legal safeguards that contribute to fostering a harmonious work/life balance.

First and foremost, understanding your rights as an employee is crucial in ensuring fair treatment in the workplace. These rights encompass a wide range of areas, including protection from discrimination, harassment, and unfair dismissal. By familiarizing yourself with these rights, you can confidently navigate your professional life, knowing that you are entitled to a safe and equitable work environment.

Moreover, legal protections play a vital role in safeguarding your work/life balance. Many jurisdictions have enacted laws to protect employees from excessive working hours and ensure adequate compensation for overtime. These regulations play a pivotal role in preventing burnout and enabling employees to maintain a healthy balance between their personal and professional lives.

Additionally, legal protections extend to parental leave and flexible working arrangements, which are paramount in achieving a harmonious work/life balance. These measures allow employees to prioritize their family responsibilities while still fulfilling their professional obligations. By embracing these legal protections, employers can create a supportive and inclusive work environment that enables employees to thrive in all aspects of their lives.

However, it is important to note that employee rights and legal protections are not always readily apparent. Therefore, it is crucial to educate yourself about the legislation and regulations that apply to your specific industry and jurisdiction. This knowledge empowers you to assert your rights and seek redress when necessary, ensuring that you are treated fairly and equitably.

In conclusion, employee rights and legal protections are fundamental to achieving a healthy work/life balance. By understanding your rights and the legal safeguards available to you, you can navigate your professional life with confidence and advocate for a work environment that supports your well-being. It is essential for employees to familiarize themselves with these rights and protections, as they are crucial in promoting a harmonious and fulfilling work/life balance.

Collaborating with employers for positive change

In today's fast-paced and demanding work environment, finding a healthy work/life balance has become more crucial than ever. As employees, we often find ourselves struggling to juggle our professional responsibilities with our personal lives, leading to stress, burnout, and a decline in overall well-being. However, there is hope. By collaborating with employers for positive change, we can create a work environment that promotes and supports a healthy work/life balance.

The importance of a healthy work/life balance cannot be overstated. It not only benefits us as individuals but also contributes to increased job satisfaction and overall productivity. When we have time to recharge and take care of our personal needs, we come back to work feeling refreshed and motivated. This, in turn, leads to higher job performance and greater engagement.

Employers play a significant role in shaping work/life balance. By recognizing the importance of this balance, they can implement policies and practices that support their employees' well-being. One way employers can collaborate with us is by offering flexible work arrangements such as remote work, flexible hours, or compressed workweeks. These options allow us to better manage our personal commitments while still meeting our professional obligations.

Moreover, employers can encourage open communication and transparency. Establishing a culture where employees feel comfortable discussing their work/life needs and concerns can lead to better understanding and more effective solutions. By actively seeking input from employees and considering their feedback, employers can continuously improve work/life balance initiatives.

Training and development programs can also contribute to a healthy work/life balance. Employers can provide resources and workshops that focus on time management, stress reduction, and work/life integration. By equipping employees with the necessary skills and tools, employers empower us to take control of our work and personal lives, ultimately fostering a better balance.

Lastly, employers can lead by example. When managers and leaders prioritize their own work/life balance, it sends a powerful message to employees. By demonstrating a commitment to self-care and setting boundaries, employers inspire us to do the same.

In conclusion, collaborating with employers for positive change is essential in achieving a healthy work/life balance. By recognizing the importance of this balance, employers can implement flexible work arrangements, foster open communication, provide training programs, and lead by example. As employees, it is essential for us to communicate our needs, advocate for our well-being, and actively engage in these collaborative efforts. Together, we can create a work environment that supports and promotes a healthy work/life balance, leading to greater satisfaction, productivity, and overall well-being.

In today's fast-paced and demanding work environment, achieving a healthy work/life balance is crucial for our overall well-being and success. As employees, we often find ourselves struggling to find the perfect equilibrium between our professional responsibilities and personal lives. However, it is important to recognize that we are not alone in this pursuit. Employers play a significant role in shaping and supporting work/life balance for their employees, making collaboration with them essential for positive change.

One of the key aspects of collaborating with employers for a healthy work/life balance is open communication. It is vital to establish a transparent dialogue with your employer about your needs and expectations. By expressing your desire for a better work/life balance, you pave the way for constructive discussions about potential solutions or adjustments that can be made. This collaboration can lead to flexible working hours, remote work options, or even the introduction of well-being programs within the workplace.

Employers have begun to recognize the importance of work/life balance in enhancing employee satisfaction and productivity. Many organizations are now actively implementing policies and initiatives to support their employees' well-being. Collaborating with employers can help ensure that these initiatives are effective and tailored to the specific needs of the workforce. By taking an active role in providing feedback and suggestions, employees can help shape these programs and policies, making them more impactful and beneficial for all.

Additionally, collaborating with employers can help create a supportive work culture that values work/life balance. By actively engaging with the organization's initiatives and advocating for positive change, employees can inspire their colleagues to prioritize their well-being as well. This collaborative effort can foster a culture of flexibility and understanding, where employees feel empowered to prioritize their personal lives without fear of negative repercussions.

Moreover, collaborating with employers allows employees to contribute to the overall success of the organization. A healthy work/life balance not only benefits individuals but also improves productivity, reduces burnout, and increases employee retention. By actively participating in the efforts to enhance work/life balance, employees can help create a positive and sustainable work environment that benefits everyone involved.

In conclusion, collaborating with employers for positive change in achieving a healthy work/life balance is essential for employees. By engaging in open communication, advocating for change, and actively participating in the organization's initiatives, employees can contribute to a work culture that values well-being and supports a balanced lifestyle. Remember, a healthy work/life balance is not just a personal goal but an essential component of overall success and happiness.

Conclusion: Empowering Employees for a Balanced Life

In this journey towards understanding the power of flexibility and work-life balance, we have explored various aspects that affect our lives as employees. We have delved into the importance of maintaining a healthy work-life balance and how it can empower us to lead a more fulfilled and satisfying life. As we conclude our exploration, it is crucial to recognize the significance of empowering ourselves in order to achieve this balance.

A healthy work-life balance is not just a necessity; it is a fundamental right that we should all strive to achieve. It allows us to nurture our personal and professional lives harmoniously, leading to better overall well-being. By prioritizing our needs and creating boundaries between work and personal life, we can enhance our productivity, creativity, and overall job satisfaction.

It is essential for employees to understand that they hold the power to shape their work-life balance. Empowerment lies in recognizing our own worth and setting realistic expectations for ourselves. It involves advocating for our needs and communicating them effectively with our employers. By engaging in open and honest conversations with our supervisors, we can negotiate flexible work arrangements that suit both our personal and professional lives.

Employers play a crucial role in empowering employees for a balanced life. Organizations that value work-life balance foster a culture of respect, trust, and open communication. They provide the necessary tools and resources to support employees in achieving this balance.

Employers can implement policies such as flexible working hours, remote work options, and wellness programs to ensure the well-being of their workforce.

As employees, we must actively participate in creating a work-life balance that meets our needs. This may involve setting boundaries and learning to disconnect from work during personal time. It also means taking care of our physical and mental health by prioritizing self-care activities such as exercise, hobbies, and spending quality time with loved ones.

In conclusion, the power to achieve a balanced life lies within each of us. By acknowledging the importance of work-life balance and empowering ourselves, we can lead happier, more fulfilling lives. Let us take charge of our own well-being and work towards creating a harmonious integration of our personal and professional lives. Remember, a balanced life is not just a dream – it is a reality that we can make possible.

In today's fast-paced and demanding work environment, achieving a healthy work/life balance has become more important than ever. As employees, we often find ourselves juggling multiple responsibilities, both at work and in our personal lives. The constant struggle to maintain harmony between these two domains can have detrimental effects on our overall well-being and happiness. However, it is crucial to remember that we have the power to change this narrative and create a more balanced life for ourselves.

Throughout this book, "The Power of Flexibility: How Employers Shape Work/Life Balance," we have explored the various aspects of work/life balance and learned how employers can play a significant role in shaping our experiences. We have discussed the importance of setting boundaries, managing time effectively, and finding ways to recharge ourselves outside of work. Now, in this concluding chapter, we will focus on empowering ourselves to take control of our work/life balance and create a more fulfilling and harmonious life.

One of the fundamental steps towards achieving a balanced life is understanding the significance of self-care. We must prioritize our physical and mental well-being by incorporating regular exercise, healthy eating, and sufficient rest into our daily routines. By taking care of ourselves, we can better handle the demands of our professional lives and reduce the risk of burnout.

Another key aspect of empowering ourselves for a balanced life is learning to communicate our needs and boundaries effectively. Open and honest conversations with our supervisors and colleagues can help establish clear expectations and prevent work from encroaching on our personal lives. It is essential to advocate for flexible work arrangements, such as remote work or flexible hours, that suit our individual needs and enable us to fulfill our personal commitments.

Moreover, we should embrace technology as a tool to enhance our work/life balance rather than letting it consume us. By utilizing productivity apps, project management tools, and communication platforms effectively, we can streamline our work processes and create more time for ourselves and our loved ones.

Ultimately, achieving a healthy work/life balance requires a proactive approach. It is up to us, as employees, to take charge of our well-being and make conscious decisions that prioritize our personal lives alongside our professional goals. By implementing the strategies and practices discussed in this book, we can create a more fulfilling and sustainable work/life balance.

Remember, a balanced life is not a luxury; it is a necessity for our overall happiness and success. Let us empower ourselves to make the necessary changes and embrace a more balanced life, where both our work and personal lives thrive harmoniously.